MY AWESOME FIELD GUIDE
TO NORTH AMERICAN BIRDS

My Awesome

FIELD GUIDE to

NORTH AMERICAN BIRDS

Find and Identify Your
Feathered Friends

MIKE GRAF

**ROCKRIDGE
PRESS**

For general information on our other products and services or to obtain technical support, please contact our Customer Care Department within the United States at (866) 744-2665, or outside the United States at (510) 253-0500.

Rockridge Press publishes its books in a variety of electronic and print formats. Some content that appears in print may not be available in electronic books, and vice versa.

TRADEMARKS: Rockridge Press and the Rockridge Press logo are trademarks or registered trademarks of Callisto Media Inc. and/or its affiliates, in the United States and other countries, and may not be used without written permission. All other trademarks are the property of their respective owners. Rockridge Press is not associated with any product or vendor mentioned in this book.

Series Designer: Josh Moore
Interior and Cover Designer: Scott Petrower
Art Producer: Sue Bischofberger
Editor: Andrea Leptinsky
Production Editor: Jenna Dutton
Production Manager: Holly Haydash

All images used under license from shutterstock.com and iStockphoto.com.

ISBN: Print 978-1-64876-354-0 | eBook 978-1-64876-355-7
R0

~~~

This book is dedicated to
Rich Gerston, a lifelong friend
and avid birder. How many
"lifers" are on your list now?

~~~

Contents

Landbirds and Songbirds

Raptors

Shorebirds

Waterbird

Waterfowl

Landbirds and Songbirds

Raptors

Shorebirds

Waterbirds

Waterfowl

Welcome, Birders!

Y ou probably can't wait to get out and go birding! This lifelong hobby will likely motivate you to slow down as you go about your day. Stop, watch, and listen to the hidden world of birds all around you.

I highly suggest you use this field notebook (see page 119) while birding, make sketches, and possibly create a birding scrapbook. The notes can help you keep a running list of the birds you've seen and the locations where you spotted them. They could also list the time of year, conditions, and weather. Your notes may include who you were with and the bird's behaviors or actions that you observed.

Use these notes to compare and contrast your birding experiences. You'll become amazed at the birds you've observed, and you'll have many stories to tell.

I have written more than 95 books for children and families. My books are all about the outdoors, including many on national parks, where my birding got started. I can still vividly recall the giant California condors I have seen—very closely, mind you—at Pinnacles National Park in California. In Grand Teton National Park, my family and I saw a strikingly orange-yellow western tanager on a guided ranger–led walk. I'll never forget the mountain bluebird that repeatedly dive-bombed me in Canyonlands National Park.

National parks are great places to start birding adventures. But don't worry; if you don't live close to one, there are many other great birding locations throughout the United States and North America, including your own backyard!

What's That Bird?

We all have seen birds. But do you know what makes a bird a *bird*?

First, birds are **vertebrates**. These are animals with backbones. We also know that most birds fly. They have light skeletons that make flying possible. Only about 40 bird species on the planet do not fly—one example is an ostrich. Birds also are the only vertebrates with feathers. They have bills or beaks, not teeth, and their bills come in a variety of shapes and sizes. And birds hatch from eggs. Birds are also **endothermic**, meaning they generate their own body heat.

Bird-watching is a popular hobby that anyone can do. Some people bird-watch just for fun. Others may want to know what kind of birds are in their yard or live in a certain **habitat**, or the natural home of a plant or animal. Some people lead tours in areas known for birds and help point them out. Finally, some bird-watchers help with scientific studies of birds or bird counts, which can tell us which birds live in certain areas, and about their **migration** patterns, or where they travel to and from.

Field marks, or visible characteristics, are keys to identifying a bird type. The four main types are a bird's color pattern, size and shape, behavior, and habitat. As you get better at birding, you will be able to combine these categories for faster, more accurate identification of the birds you spot.

This following section explores these items in more depth.

Where Birds Come From

The Jurassic period, the grand age of dinosaurs, was 200 million to 145 million years ago. During this time, birds evolved from meat-eating dinosaurs called **theropods**, such as the T. rex. Bird fossils have been dated to 150 million years ago. These fossils show that birds are really **avian** dinosaurs. *Avian* means "related to birds."

Around 140 million years ago, the age of the dinosaurs ended. Why did birds survive? Most likely it was because of their small size, their ability to fly, and the fact that they could eat a variety of foods. Millions of years ago, birds had sharp teeth. Since then, birds have gone through many **adaptions**, or changes that help them survive.

What do present-day birds have in common with extinct dinosaurs? It turns out quite a bit. Both have feathers and lay eggs. Both have scales. Bird feathers are produced by cells similar to scales, and birds have scales on their feet. And birds and dinosaurs have some similar skeletal characteristics, such as large eye openings in their heads, hollow bones, four toes with three main toes, stiffened tails, S-shaped necks, and many more similarities.

Today, there are about 18,000 species of birds on earth, and about 2,000 of them are in North America. Each kind of bird is a **species**. A species is a form, or group, of similar living things.

Birds of the same species, of course, look similar. But males and females, as well as adults and **juveniles**, or young birds, can each look very different within the same species. Even same-species birds living in different regions of the country can have some subtle, and not-so-subtle, differences.

Using this guide will help you learn to identify each type of bird!

Bird Anatomy

Anatomy is the bodily structure and workings of an animal.

The basic outer parts of a bird are its head and bill, throat, back, breast, wings, tail, legs, and feet. All birds have two legs, two wings, feathers, and a bill. Birds also have two eyes and ears, though the ears may not be visible. Birds have a compact body shape that helps them fly. But beyond that, birds vary in size, shape, color, and patterns.

Bird heads have several features. First, they vary in shape and color. Some bird heads have crowns; stripes; a **crest**, or tuft of feathers; patches; and eye rings, or a ring of feathers that surround the eye.

Bird bills also come in a variety of shapes and colors. Birds also have different colors on their chins, necks, throats, backs, and wings. In addition, wing size and shape varies per bird.

A bird's chest is known as the **breast**. It is often a different color from the bird's back. Bird **flanks**, or sides, are between their wings and abdomen. A bird's **rump** is the patch above the tail and below the back. These may also be colored differently. Birds also have varied lengths, colors, and shapes of their tails. Tails are often held in various positions, depending on the type of bird. Bird legs and feet vary in length and color.

WHAT THE PECK?

Have you ever been outside or in a park or forest and heard loud tapping on a tree? You look up and see a woodpecker pecking away. The woodpecker is trying to get at food using its strong, sharp bill to drill into the wood.

Birds use their bills to help them get food. A hummingbird's bill is extremely long and thin, which makes it possible for them to get to nectar deep inside flowers. Raptor bills are curved, allowing them to tear into the meat of their prey.

Birds also use their bills to build nests and feed their young. Bills help birds make sounds that attract mates or announce territory.

Each bill type is an adaptation, or way that the birds have **evolved**, or changed over time to survive and thrive.

The Canada goose's bill has formations inside it made of **cartilage**. Cartilage is a tough, semitransparent, elastic tissue. These ridge-like structures help the goose pull up plants from the ground or water.

How to Identify Birds

Have you ever wondered what are the types of birds you see in your backyard? How many kinds have you seen in your whole life? Were some of the birds similar? Was it easy to tell each bird apart?

People who keep track of birds are called "birders."

Identifying birds can be tricky. Birds are recognizable by what are called "field marks." There are several key field marks that can help us recognize birds. These include the shape of the bird's head, body, bill, wings, and legs. Field marks can also be color patterns on their feathers. Finally, what each bird acts like and where the bird lives are also field marks.

How birds fly also helps you identify them. Some birds flap their wings a few times and then glide. Others, like hummingbirds, beat their wings rapidly. Some birds **hover**, or stay in one spot, while others may perform somersaults in the air. And some birds spend a large part of their time on the ground.

Birds also act differently. Some race around trying to find insects. They may bob their tails. And some also seek a certain location for protection or food.

Many birders listen for calls to identify the bird. These vocalizations are sometimes the only way to know a bird is nearby. An owl calling at night is an example of one of these times.

Where the bird lives, or its habitat, is another way to identify it. Does it dwell in the forest, near water, in the desert, or along the coast?

Birds are typically classified as small, medium, or large. Hummingbirds are small. Condors are large. There is some middle ground, though. American robins are small to medium. Spotted owls are medium to large.

If you are far away from the bird, compare it to something you know. Is the bird about the size of a pine cone? Or the size of your fist? Comparing the size of a bird to a familiar object will give you an idea of how big the bird is.

Noting the size of a bird will help you identify it.

Dove Finch Sparrow

Warbler Jay Wren

Swallow Cardinal

Crow

Duck Hawk

COLOR PATTERN

You may only see a bird for a brief second or two. One way to try to identify it is to note its colors. Is the bird light or dark? Multicolored? **Mottled**, or a spotted mix? Are the colors bold and striking or faint and subtle?

Some birds have distinct colors. Western tanagers are strikingly black, white, and yellow with some orange.

White-crowned sparrows are more subtle, but they clearly have a white crown on their head.

A bird's color patterns are one of its field marks, which, as we've read, are characteristics used to identify species. More on that later.

BEHAVIOR

Bird **behaviors** are the actions the bird takes as it reacts to the world around it. Noticing these behaviors can help guide identification.

How is the bird perched? Upright? Hunched? Is its tail sticking up? Does it stay in one place or move around? Is it flicking up leaves on the ground? Is it storing seeds in its throat or in a **cache** in a tree? Is the bird on a branch alone or hidden in the bushes? Does it travel in a flock?

House wrens are known to go into other nests and pierce the eggs. Now, that's some behavior!

HABITAT

Birds have four essentials they get from their habitat: food, water, shelter, and nesting sites. Bird habitats can include deserts; forested areas; grasslands; ocean shorelines; **tundras**, or treeless plains, like the Arctic; and wetlands. Birds also live in cities and urban areas.

Some birds migrate, or move from place to place, as food sources, water, or changing weather determine their needs. And some birds have a **range** of habitats. Ravens can live in the south, where it is warm, as well as the north, where it is colder, for example.

Knowing a bird's habitat and range can help you identify the bird.

FIELD MARKS

Field marks are the unique physical characteristics of each type of bird. Field marks include the bird's coloring and patterns all over its body. Each's bird's size, shape, bill type, and body posture are also field marks, as well as the bird's behaviors and flight patterns.

Is the bird slender and long? Small and round? Does it have long or short legs? These distinct characteristics, unique to each bird, can help us identify them.

The more you learn how to spot field marks on birds, the better you will become at knowing the type of bird you've spotted!

COLOR

One excellent way to determine a bird's type is to note standout field mark colors.

The red breast of an American robin is such an example. Another is the distinct raspberry color on the head, breast, and back of the purple finch. The tail of a red-tailed hawk also stands out for its red color.

A bird's colors are not just limited to its body. The bird's bill may be a certain color, or its eye, or its rump. In many cases, birds are noted for one color. But for some, it's a combination of colors you are looking for.

HEAD

The characteristics of a bird's head are field marks.

Features to look for are the shape, size, and color of the bill. Also, observe whether the bird has an eyeline, or a line through the eye. Some birds may have an eyebrow stripe over the eye, or an eye ring around the eye. You may even notice the bird's eye coloring as a field mark. Look for a crown stripe on its head and a crest, or tuft of feathers as well. The Steller's jay, for example, has a large, spiked crest on top of its head.

BODY

Birds, like humans, have differently shaped bodies. Bird bodies include parts of their wings, wing tips, neck, back, rump, flank or sides, shoulders, legs and feet, and underside, or breast.

Bird bodies are classified as small, medium, or large. Bird bodies may be long and thin, or they might be plump and round. Some birds may look puffed up.

An example of a unique body is the broad-shouldered and plump-shaped American woodcock.

All these body characteristics are part of the bird's field marks and help with identification.

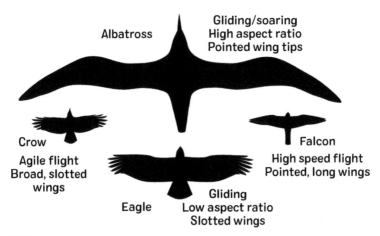

Albatross
Gliding/soaring
High aspect ratio
Pointed wing tips

Crow
Agile flight
Broad, slotted wings

Falcon
High speed flight
Pointed, long wings

Eagle
Gliding
Low aspect ratio
Slotted wings

TAIL

Bird tails have different functions. They are used to steer while in flight, to brake or slow down while landing, to sustain lift on updrafts, to balance upright while perched, and to show emotion, among other things.

There are six shapes that a bird's tails may have: fanned out, forked, notched, pointed, rounded, or square tipped. When observing a bird's tail, note whether the tail is long or short. Does it stick up? What color is the tail? Is it banded or striped?

The northern pintail duck has a standout tail field mark. Its tail is exceptionally long and pointed.

Birds have primary flight feathers that help the bird thrust forward and secondary feathers that help provide lift. Birds keep their wings flat while flying, which allows air to go around the wings. When they go forward, air is pushed up from below. This is how birds are able to fly.

Turkey vultures often glide high up in the sky while soaring in circles. Turkey vultures teeter, or wobble, back and forth while gliding. This is a unique flight pattern.

The much smaller ruby-crowned kinglet uses a flight technique called **hawking**. Hawking, the act of a bird catching prey in the air with its bill, occurs when a bird flies up from a perch and then back again in a circular pattern. This helps them catch insects.

Some birds hover, which is when a bird stays put in one spot for a period of time. Hummingbirds often do this.

Owls fly silently at night. This helps them catch their prey. Owls have special feathers that allow them to absorb noise and alter air patterns.

Other types of bird flight include flying in a direct line, flap-and-glide rotations, soaring in circles, straight-line and V-formation flying in groups, and **undulating**, or roller coaster–like flying where you observe the bird rising and falling.

What about speed? The world's slowest flying bird is the American woodcock, topping out at 5 miles per hour. The fastest flying birds are peregrine falcons.

When they tuck their wings and dive, they can reach speeds of 250 miles per hour!

SOUNDS AND SONGS

Sometimes while birding, you can hear birds but not see them. They may be singing or just calling.

About half of the world's 18,000 species of birds are songbirds. Bird songs and calls can mean a variety of things. Early in the morning is the best time to hear birds singing.

Bird use songs to claim territory, announcing to others nearby that they are already there. Males may also sing to attract a mate. Birds may use calls just to mark their location to other birds. Songs are typically longer than calls, with a structured pattern of vocalizing. Calls are short and not as rhythmic.

A few examples of bird calls include the great horned owl's distinct "hoo-hoo," which is a clear giveaway that one is nearby. The red-tailed hawk makes a hoarse, high-pitched, screechy "kee-eeee . . . arr" call. We know Canada geese are overhead by their honks, barks, and cackles. Perhaps one of the most recognized bird sounds is the quacking of a female mallard duck.

Males do most of the singing. Some songs are sung over and over. The veery makes one of the most pleasant of all bird songs. They repeat a "veer" sound over and over but vary its pitch. The yellow warbler sings a cheerful song, which can be recognized by comparing the rhythm and sound to the words "sweet . . . sweet . . . sweet. I'm so sweet."

The more you bird, the more you will start recognizing a variety of bird calls and songs!

An **adult** is an animal that is fully grown or developed. A **juvenile** is an animal that is *not* fully grown or developed. Just like humans, juvenile birds often look very different from adults!

Baby birds are easy to identify. They seem to have eyes and bills that are too big for their heads. They may beg for food, draw attention to their parents, and be unsteady in flight.

Juvenile birds are harder to identify. They are stubbier and shorter than adults. Colors in juveniles may also be duller than those of an adult, but they may still show some similar field marks to an adult, especially on their wings and tail.

Adult male red-winged blackbirds are glossy black with a red shoulder patch. Females are dark brown above and streaked white and brown below. Juvenile males and females look like adult females.

Juvenile bald eagles don't look "bald" until they are about five years old.

DIFFERENCES BETWEEN MALE AND FEMALE BIRDS

In the bird world, males often are more colorful. The simple reason for this is males are trying to get the attention of females to mate and create more birds.

Males try to attract females by showing off their colors. And females prefer males that are more colorful for mates. Females may even believe that a more colorful male means a healthier male.

Males also announce their territory by displaying their colors. In addition, male colors show other birds that this is their species.

As for females being duller in color? This actually helps them remain camouflaged while in the nest, protecting both the mother bird and her hatchlings.

Male northern cardinals, for example, are brilliant red except for small parts of their faces, necks, and wings. Females are mostly pale brown with just a few small spots of red. Male mallard ducks have a distinct bright green head. Females are mostly mottled brown.

EGGS-CELLENT!

In addition to the birds themselves, bird eggs are varied in shape. A sandpiper's eggs are shaped like teardrops. Owl eggs are golf ball–shaped. Hummingbird eggs are like jelly beans.

The egg shapes can determine what kind of flyer the bird will be. Good flyers, like the sandpiper, typically have **elongated**—or longer, oval-shaped—eggs. New research tells us that the better a bird is at flying, and specifically the length and width of the bird's wing, correlates to the type of eggs the bird lays. Good flyers need compact, lightweight bodies, which means less space inside their bodies for the eggs. So these birds—birds that are strong flyers—have elongated and pointier eggs to fit inside their narrower bodies.

Birds that spend little time in the air often have **spherical**, or round, eggs. The guillemot has pear-shaped eggs, which are a lot less likely to roll off the cliffs where these birds nest.

Bird eggs have different colors, too. Darker eggs are harder to spot and the darker colors may also guard the baby bird inside against infection, or help keep the growing chick warm. Speckled eggs, which may also be better camouflaged, typically have thinner shells and are laid by perching birds. Another reason for bird egg colors? So the parents can recognize an intruder egg that has been dumped in their nest in the hopes that these new "parents" will raise the chick.

Let's Look for Birds

L et's get ready to go birding!

First, plan ahead. Where do you want to go? A park? By a lake or river? Near the ocean? Or possibly even into your backyard? These are all good locations with unique habitats for birds. Also, many birders feel that mornings are the most active time for birds and the best time to observe them.

This section of the book will tell you where to look for birds and when. You'll also learn what to bring with you and how to use this field guide and notebook journal to help you along the way.

Keep in mind, every time you go out birding, you will see different things. Once you get started, you may develop a lifelong hobby!

Where to Find Birds

Think about where you live. Are you close to any natural areas, such as rivers, parks, or forests? Do you live near the ocean? Many birders like to start their bird-watching in nature preserves, where you are more likely to see birds in their natural habitat.

You can also start bird-watching right in your own backyard. Do you have trees or flowers that attract birds? Can you place a feeder outside and bring birds to you? More on that later.

There are hundreds of national wildlife refuges across the country. Many of them are great bird habitats. Find out if any are near your home area. State and national parks, and national monuments and preserves are also good locations for bird-watching. Websites, such as the National Audubon Society and Ebird, might also list some great places to see birds near where you live.

If you can't travel, starting at or near your house is an easy option. Do your trees and bushes attract birds? Look for areas where birds might perch in the morning, such as tree snags, power lines, and fence posts.

The birds you also see in any of these environments might be affected by their range. Range is the limit of distance where a bird might live. In other words, you might see some birds seasonally, only as they migrate, or travel, from place to place. The birds you view likely are affected by the food sources nearby. If you see a bird, there is likely food for them somewhere close.

Habitat

Birds, like all animals, live in varied habitats. Birds choose different habitats based on food sources, safety from predators, areas to nest, and availability of water.

One of the four habitats covered in this book is an aquatic one. **Aquatic** means in or near water. Aquatic habitats include lakes, ponds, streams, and wetlands. This type of habitat can also include irrigated farms. Aquatic birds may be at the beach or on coastal islands and **sea stacks**, which are towers of rocks jutting out near the ocean's shoreline.

The second of the four habitats is woodlands. Woodlands are forested areas mostly filled with trees. The forests provide food, water, and shelter for the birds that live there.

The third type of habitat is grasslands. These are open areas with few or no trees, but with meadows and grassy areas. Grasslands are not deserts, as grasslands get more rain. Birds that live in these areas are often ground feeders. And there aren't typically places to hide from predators. Almost half the earth is grassland habitat.

The fourth habitat is shrub areas. These are places with short, sometimes thick plants and bushes, or thickets. Some areas in the desert may be like this. **Urban**, or city-like, locations may be as well. Birds found in this type of habitat often hide out in the thickets.

Range

A bird's range covers the places it lives during its lifetime. Some birds are typically found in one area and have a very small range. Others migrate based on seasonal weather and the availability of food, and their range is very large. Knowing this helps you understand which birds can be found during various times of the year in different habitats.

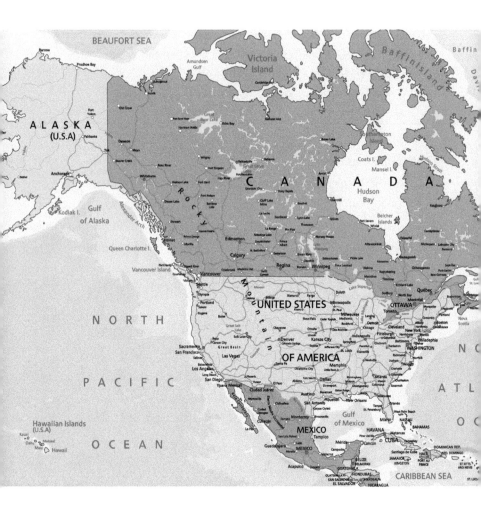

The American robin has a broad, year-round range and is commonly seen all over North America. The robin does not need to migrate during winter because it can tolerate very cold weather and find food.

The California condor, on the other hand, has a limited range. Condors once roamed the skies across all of the Southwest and parts of Texas. But in the 1980s, these magnificent birds almost went **extinct**. Now they are being reintroduced into a few select areas near the California coast and in parts of Nevada, Utah, and Arizona.

Some birds are what are called **altitude**, or elevation, migrants. They don't fly to different regions for warmer weather, but just change elevation seasonally. The yellow-eyed junco, greater sage-grouse, prairie falcon, and American dipper are some North American birds known to go from low elevations in winter to the high mountains in summer.

The champion of migration is the Arctic tern. The Arctic tern breeds in the Arctic and flies all the way to the Southern Hemisphere in summer, then returns to the Arctic. That is about 24,000 miles of flight per year! Talk about a frequent flyer.

Migration

Some birds migrate; others stay in one area and are called **residents**. Migration is the seasonal movement of animals from one region to another. This typically occurs in spring or fall, and this is a great time to bird-watch. In these seasons, birders are more likely to spot migratory birds, or birds moving from place to place, not seen at other times of the year.

Birds migrate as **resources**, or things they need to live, decrease in one area and increase in another. For some North American birds, as winter approaches, food becomes scarcer, so they move south. This, in turn, happens again when they move north for summer.

About 40 percent of all birds migrate. Even emperor penguins migrate—though they do it by marching on land. Migrating birds travel **flyways**, which are north-to-south migration routes between their nesting and wintering areas.

Most birds migrate by instinct. As the seasonal hours of daylight change, their instincts kick in.

Migrating birds are sensitive to Earth's magnetic fields, which help lead them to their final destination. Some birds navigate using the Sun and stars, and some acquire the knowledge needed for the journey from their parents and other older birds.

These journeys can take a long time—but birds can sleep while flying! They keep one eye open and still carry on their quests.

Birds can succumb to storms along the way, but most survive. Small birds may seek shelter near trees and hedges. If they stay near the ground, the temperatures there may be warmer. And bird feathers actually trap warm, dry air around the bird and help prevent the cold and wet air from coming in.

Pacific Flyway

Atlantic Flyway

Mississippi Flyway

Central Flyway

COMMON SEASONAL BIRDS

	SPRING	SUMMER
1.	American goldfinch	American crow
2.	American robin	American goldfinch
3.	Brewer's blackbird	American robin
4.	Common grackle	Barn swallow
5.	Eastern phoebe	Blue jay
6.	European starling	House finch
7.	Killdeer	Mourning dove
8.	Northern cardinal	Northern cardinal
9.	Red-winged blackbird	Song sparrow
10.	Tree swallow	Turkey vulture

COMMON SEASONAL BIRDS

FALL	WINTER
American tree sparrow	American goldfinch
Bald eagle	American robin
Black-capped chickadee	Blue jay
Eastern bluebird	Canada goose
Mourning dove	Dark-eyed junco
Pine siskin	Downy woodpecker
Prairie falcon	European starling
Trumpeter swan	House finch
Tufted titmouse	Mallard
White-breasted nuthatch	Northern cardinal

If you can't go out into the wild to see birds, you might consider bringing the birds to you.

By following some simple techniques, you should be able to look out the window and watch bird action unfold. Who is coming to the feeder? Are there a variety of birds? Do you see returning birds? Do certain foods work better than others?

Perhaps the best way to get birds to come by is to set up a feeder. There are several types that can be bought or made. You'll want to construct the feeder so you'll be able to clean it easily, refill the food, and observe the birds that eat at the feeder.

Another way to get birds into your yard is to build a birdhouse. Birds that use birdhouses typically build nests in sheltered areas. You'll want to consider adding elements to your birdhouse to attract birds, such as food, water, and nesting material. Try to place the birdhouse in a private, natural area.

Birds need fresh water for drinking and bathing. Setting up a birdbath at ground level with shallow or gently running water that mimics nature seems to be what birds like best.

The internet has a number of great websites that can help you learn how to build or buy bird feeders, houses, or baths. These sites can also give you more ideas on how to attract birds to your backyard.

COMMON FEEDER BIRDS

Once you have your feeder set up, you can start watching who shows up to eat. Depending on the season, where you live, and what food you use, you'll hopefully start getting guests right away.

Here is a list of some of the most commonly seen birds that come to feeders in the United States:

American crow

American goldfinch

American robin

Baltimore oriole

Black-billed magpie

Black-capped chickadee

Black-chinned hummingbird

Blue jay

Common grackle

Dark-eyed junco

Downy woodpecker

European starling

House finch

House sparrow

Mourning dove

Northern cardinal

Pine grosbeak

Pine siskin

Red-winged blackbird

Rosy-finch

Spotted towhee

Tufted titmouse

Western meadowlark

White-breasted nuthatch

Yellow-rumped warbler

Once you are in the ideal location for spotting birds, you'll want to be an active observer. Do you want to stay in one place or move around? Also, try to stay quiet and at a distance.

Record what you see by sketching drawings or taking photos. Try to keep a running list of bird types and a log of the date, time, and location spotted, so you can add to your journal each time you go out.

Here are some more tips you can use to get the most out of birding:

→ Look at the bird, not the field guide. Seconds later, the bird may be gone, but the field guide will still be there.

→ Try to get a general impression of the bird. Consider field marks such as size, shape, color, and unusual features.

→ Pick a good spot. Location, location, location!

→ Be patient. Birding takes time.

→ Try to see if you can spot familiar birds. There may be a certain bird you've seen before and can spot easily.

→ The saying "The early bird gets the worm" really applies to birding!

→ Consider the time of year. The birds you see can vary depending on where you live, the season, and possible migration patterns in your area.

→ The less the birds see of you, the better the birding. Avoid bright clothes.

→ Practice spotting and identifying birds out your window or as you go about your day.

→ Avoid sudden movements that might startle the birds.

WHAT YOU NEED IN THE FIELD

Now that it is time to go birding, you'll want to have the right supplies with you. Here are some things you'll need:

→ Field guide for the area in which you're birding, showing a list of birds that live in that area

→ Binoculars or spotting scopes, and extras if you are birding with others

→ Hat and sunscreen—total sun protection

→ Water and food—in case you stay out longer than planned

→ Layers of clothes to fit expected and unexpected weather

→ Pencil, pen, and possibly a sketchbook and journal for keeping records of birds seen

→ Camera

→ Connect with groups—possibly join others for the outing

→ Apps—smartphone applications for instant field guide identification of birds and sounds

→ This book, of course!

One of the most important items you can bring along for proper birding is a pair of binoculars. Binoculars will make colors stand out as well as enhance features such as a bird's bill or head crown. Some birders say that binoculars are an extension of their eyes when out observing.

The correct binoculars for birding have important features. You'll want a pair with a central focus wheel as well as a **diopter** focus, which allows both eyes to see equally.

All binoculars are labeled with a pair of numbers, such as 8x45. The first number is the power. Power means how much larger the object being viewed is to our naked eye. If it says 8, then what we see through the lens is 8 times larger than what we would see without the binoculars. The second number is the diameter, or width, of the front lens closest to the bird. This helps make the object appear clearer and lighter. Birders usually prefer 8x or 10x magnification: 10x is better for distance birding, but with 8x, you can get a wider image that is easier to follow moving birds with.

When spotting a bird, focus on nonmoving features around the bird that you can pick out using your binoculars. Then lift the binoculars toward your eyes while you are staring at the bird and look for that spot. This way you—hopefully—don't lose the bird.

How to Use This Field Guide

The following section of this book is your field guide to the North American birds you are most likely to see.

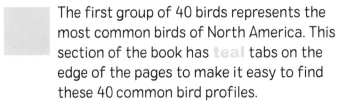

The first group of 40 birds represents the most common birds of North America. This section of the book has teal tabs on the edge of the pages to make it easy to find these 40 common bird profiles.

The second group of birds covers 110 other common North American backyard birds—and beyond. These pages have **red** tabs on the side of the pages so you can distinguish this section from the 40 most common birds when looking something up.

All the birds, regardless of category, are further identified within five subgroups, indicated by a colored tab on the page:

A yellow tab will tell you the bird is waterfowl, which are birds who spend their non-flying time on water. These include ducks and geese, and sometimes swans, coots, and grebes, too.

Orange means the bird is a waterbird. Waterbirds live around water and like to go swimming, but they don't necessarily spend all their time in the water (like waterfowl do).

Blue classifies a shorebird, or a bird found near the ocean's shoreline.

Green tells you the bird is a songbird and/ or landbird. Songbirds—birds whose calls are made up of musical tones—are the most common type of bird. Landbirds are birds that dwell in trees, perch on posts, and feed on the ground. Although this definition could include raptors, they have their own category (see the pink tab).

Pink tabs identify the bird as a **raptor**— a bird of prey such as an eagle, hawk, falcon, or owl. These birds are noted for their hooked bills and sharp talons.

The colored tabs also have symbols beneath them to help you locate and identify your bird's habitat. Know that some birds overlap into two or more habitats:

A wave symbol indicates that the bird is aquatic and lives near water.

A tree symbol shows that the bird likely dwells in a wooded area.

A grass symbol means that the bird lives in open grasslands.

A shrub symbol means that the bird typically lives in shrubs and sometimes in urban, or city, areas.

A fact sheet is a short, compact list of the most identifiable features of a bird or list of birds. Birders can use these sheets to help identify birds in the field. When observing the bird, note its features on the sheet to determine what bird you are looking at.

In addition to the colored tabs for the two sections, the fact sheets about each bird are also organized into color-coded categories, as well as by symbols. This will help you find the right section to look up a bird quickly and easily.

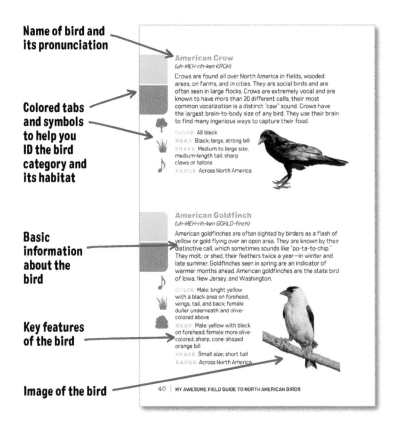

Name of bird and its pronunciation

Colored tabs and symbols to help you ID the bird category and its habitat

Basic information about the bird

Key features of the bird

Image of the bird

American Crow
(uh-MEH-rih-ken KROH)

Crows are found all over North America in fields, wooded areas, on farms, and in cities. They are social birds and are often seen in large flocks. Crows are extremely vocal and are known to have more than 20 different calls; their most common vocalization is a distinct "caw" sound. Crows have the largest brain-to-body size of any bird. They use their brain to find many ingenious ways to capture their food.

COLOR: All black
HEAD: Black; large, strong bill
SHAPE: Medium to large size, medium-length tail; sharp claws or talons
RANGE: Across North America

American Goldfinch
(uh-MEH-rih-ken GOHLD-finch)

American goldfinches are often sighted by birders as a flash of yellow or gold flying over an open area. They are known by their distinctive call, which sometimes sounds like "po-ta-to-chip." They molt, or shed, their feathers twice a year—in winter and late summer. Goldfinches seen in spring are an indicator of warmer months ahead. American goldfinches are the state bird of Iowa, New Jersey, and Washington.

COLOR: Male: bright yellow with a black area on forehead, wings, tail, and back; female duller underneath and olive-colored above
HEAD: Male: yellow with black on forehead; female: more olive-colored; sharp, cone-shaped orange bill
SHAPE: Small size; short tail
RANGE: Across North America

40 | MY AWESOME FIELD GUIDE TO NORTH AMERICAN BIRDS

There are about 2,000 different kinds of birds seen in North America. Many of them can be observed across the whole continent. Some birds live only in certain parts of North America, such as the western half or in northern locations. And some birds are in isolated regions, such as deserts or coastal areas.

Because of this fact, when observing birds, you are more likely to see some birds than others. As explained earlier, the first part of the following section, identified by teal-tabbed pages, is a field guide to 40 of the most common birds seen across North America. It is best to identify common birds first before trying to spot lesser-known species.

The second section, marked by red-tabbed pages, consists of 110 other birds seen throughout North America. These birds are less likely to be seen than the 40 most common birds, but patient birders still have a good chance of spotting them.

Field Guide: Common Birds

American Crow
(uh-MEH-rih-ken KROH)

Crows are found all over North America in fields, wooded areas, on farms, and in cities. They are social birds and are often seen in large flocks. Crows are extremely vocal and are known to have more than 20 different calls; their most common vocalization is a distinct "caw" sound. Crows have the largest brain-to-body size of any bird. They use their brain to find many ingenious ways to capture their food.

COLOR: All black

HEAD: Black; large, strong bill

SHAPE: Medium to large size; medium-length tail; sharp claws or talons

RANGE: Across North America

American Goldfinch
(uh-MEH-rih-ken GOHLD-finch)

American goldfinches are often sighted by birders as a flash of yellow or gold flying over an open area. They are known by their distinctive call, which sometimes sounds like "po-ta-to-chip." They molt, or shed, their feathers twice a year—in winter and late summer. Goldfinches seen in spring are an indicator of warmer months ahead. American goldfinches are the state bird of Iowa, New Jersey, and Washington.

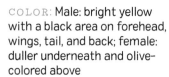

COLOR: Male: bright yellow with a black area on forehead, wings, tail, and back; female: duller underneath and olive-colored above

HEAD: Male: yellow with black on forehead; female: more olive-colored; sharp, cone-shaped orange bill

SHAPE: Small size; short tail

RANGE: Across North America

American Robin
(uh-MEH-rih-ken RAH-bin)

American robins are found all over North America. Both the male and female have orange bellies, but males are a brighter orange color and have a brighter-colored bill and black head. Robins typically stand upright and hop from place to place searching for food such as insects and berries. Robins wake up early and are often the first birds heard singing cheerfully in the morning—sometimes even before daylight!

COLOR: Orange belly and black head

HEAD: Black; bright orange bill; males have a white ring around the eyes

SHAPE: Small to medium size; large, round body; long legs; roundish tail

RANGE: Across North America

Barn Swallow
(BAARN SWAA-loh)

Barn swallows fly inches above the ground or water in search of food. They catch insects and eat them while in the air. Barn swallows build nests that are made of mud and shaped like a cup. They are aggressive birds and will chase away large birds from their nests. Some barn swallows migrate from North America south to Argentina, almost 5,600 miles away!

COLOR: Glistening cobalt blue above and light brown underneath; throat and forehead are rusty-brown-colored

HEAD: Round; small bill

SHAPE: Small; broad shoulders with pointed wings

RANGE: Breed in North America; Central and South America in winter

Black-Capped Chickadee
(BLAK kapt CHI-kuh-dee)

Black-capped chickadees are commonly seen in wooded areas shared with other types of birds. Chickadees have a varied diet that includes seeds, berries, and plants. They also devour insects, as well as meat and nuts. Chickadees are highly active and known for their "chick-a dee" call. Chickadees are easy to attract to home feeders and will often take away one seed at a time and stuff them into crevices in trees for storage.

COLOR: White bodies; black cap on head and underneath chin; white underbelly

HEAD: Roundish

SHAPE: Small size; small, black, short beak; long tail

RANGE: Most areas of the northern half of the United States

Blue Jay
(bloo jay)

Blue jays are noisy birds. Blue jays are **omnivores** and what they eat depends on the time of year. They'll eat seeds, nuts, and grains, the eggs of other birds, baby birds, and insects. Blue jays love acorns, and because of that, they are a possible reason for the spread of oak trees across the continent. Blue jays can mimic hawk calls, sometimes even confusing bird-watchers.

COLOR: Mostly blue above and white underneath with some black streaks; black ring around neck; tails are blue, black, and white

HEAD: Crested; medium-size, thick beak

SHAPE: Medium size; black legs; long tail

RANGE: Eastern two-thirds of the United States; the Pacific Northwest

Brown-Headed Cowbird
(brown HEH-did KOW-burd)

The brown-headed cowbird is most known for how it raises its young. Females don't build nests, but lay dozens of eggs in summer. They lay these eggs, however, in the nests of other birds, hoping those birds will raise their young—with their chicks or even instead of their own chicks. Cowbirds live in open, grassy areas that have few trees. They roost with other species of blackbirds, often in areas with thousands of birds.

COLOR: Male: black body and brown head; female: plain brown though lighter underneath

HEAD: Round; thick, cone-shaped bill

SHAPE: Small to medium size; stocky build

RANGE: Across southern United States

Cedar Waxwing
(SEE-dr WAKS-wing)

Cedar waxwings are colorful birds. They stay low in bushes, and with their loud, whistling-like call, they are sometimes heard before they are seen. Waxwings prefer living in forested areas, especially near streams. Cedar waxwings get their name from the cedar berries they like to eat in winter. They are also named for their waxy, red-colored wing tips.

COLOR: Black mask across eyes and head; pale-yellow belly; yellow tip of tail; wings with red tips

HEAD: Brown cap color on head; feathers that spike up, or crest

SHAPE: Small; has a large chest

RANGE: Breeds in Canada; seen across the United States

Common Grackle
(KAA-muhn GRA-kl)

Common grackles are blackbirds. Their bodies are long and thin, giving them an appearance of being stretched out. They are often seen near farming areas, where they forage for food such as grains or rice. Grackles are noisy birds. Grackles will allow ants to crawl on them. The ants secrete, or emit, an acid that kills parasites. This is called **anting**.

COLOR: Male: dark with a bluish-green tint on the head, bronze body; female: less glossy

HEAD: Oval to flat-shaped; long bill; pale-yellow eyes

SHAPE: Small to medium size; thin and tall; long legs and tail

RANGE: East Coast to the Rocky Mountains

Dark-Eyed Junco
(DAARK eye-d JUHNH-koh)

Dark-eyed juncos breed mostly in Canada, then come to North America for the winter. They hop on the ground looking for food and will search among twigs and leaves for insects. While flying, they pump their tails, causing the white part underneath to flash in the light. Dark-eyed juncos are nicknamed "snowbirds." They puff up and grow more feathers in winter. Juncos can live a long time, up to 11 years.

COLOR: White tail feathers; male: mostly gray with white belly; female: paler than the male, brownish-gray above

HEAD: Round; small, pale-colored bill

SHAPE: Small size; long tail

RANGE: Breeds often in Canada; overwinters in the United States; prefers forested areas

Downy Woodpecker
(DOW-nee WUHD-peh-kr)

Downy woodpeckers are the smallest woodpecker in America. They are found along streams and in wooded areas, as well as in city parks. Downy woodpeckers nest in holes inside trees. They have two forward- and two rear-facing toes, as well as sharp claws. This allows them to move along branches, stems, and tree trunks easily. They may even peck away for insects and larvae while dangling upside down.

COLOR: Male: black with white spots; red spot on back of head; female: no red spot on head; white to brownish-gray underneath; black and white stripes on body and head

HEAD: Short, sharp bills

SHAPE: Small to medium size

RANGE: Across the United States

Eurasian Collared-Dove
(yur-AY-zhan KAA-lard DUV)

The Eurasian collared-dove gets its name from the black collar on its neck. This bird is not native to the United States but was brought to the Bahamas in the 1970s. They made it to Florida 10 years later and have spread across the country since then. The male coos, sometimes all day long, hoping for a mate. Males will fly straight up, clap their wings, then descend with their tail spread, hoping to attract a female.

COLOR: Mostly sandy-brown-colored all over; black collar on the back of the neck

HEAD: Small for the body's size

SHAPE: Medium size; long, square, tipped tail

RANGE: Year-round across North America except for the Sierra Nevada Mountains in California

European Starling
(yur-uh-PEE-uhn STAAR-ling)

European starlings were brought to the United States by Europeans in the 1890s. They were first released in New York City's Central Park. They now live all over the continent. Starlings are omnivores, eating both plants and insects. They stab their bills into the ground in search of food. Starlings compete with bluebirds and woodpeckers for nesting sites. Males are known for imitating the calls of other birds.

COLOR: Mostly black but with bits of blue-green and purple; orange legs

HEAD: Distinct, large yellow- to orange-colored pointed bills

SHAPE: Small to medium size; stocky; short tail; triangular-shaped wings

RANGE: Abundant across North America

House Finch
(hows finch)

House finches are native to the western United States and Hawaii. They were illegally sold in New York–area pet shops until 1940, when a small number were let out of cages in Long Island, New York. They now live in cities, in the country, and around farms. Males stand out due to their distinct red heads and breasts. House finches eat mostly seeds, which they crack open in their short, cone-shaped beak, but will also eat flower buds and fruit.

COLOR: Male: red around the face and upper breast, streaky brown back; female: brown overall with blurred belly colors and a streaky tail

HEAD: Thick, cone-shaped bill

SHAPE: Small size; plump and round; long tail

RANGE: Across the United States.

House Sparrow
(hows SPEH-roh)

House sparrows are so named because they often nest near homes and buildings. Living near people helps keep them safe. They also are often seen near livestock. House sparrows eat almost all grains and seeds, which includes food given to farm animals. But they'll also catch insects, even some that gather near lights in the evening.

COLOR: Male: gray crown with white cheeks and black bib; female: black and brown stripes; white underneath

HEAD: Flat; short, thick, sharply pointed bill; black patch around eye and bill

SHAPE: Small size; stocky

RANGE: Across North America

House Wren
(hows ren)

House wrens are lively, enthusiastic songbirds. They zip along in shrubs and the lower parts of trees searching for insects. House wrens are plump and round with a thin tail. They can live at sea level and up in the mountains at 10,000 feet. House wrens are known for nesting in humanmade items such as old cans, boots, and boxes, and around buildings. Males build several nests hoping to lure a female to mate.

COLOR: Mostly brown but pale at the throat; barred, darker colorings on wings

HEAD: Gentle oval shape; thin, sharp bill

SHAPE: Small size; plump and round; short tail

RANGE: Breeds throughout the United States; migrates to the southern United States and Mexico in winter

Mourning Dove
(MOR-ning DUV)

Mourning doves are found all over North America, living on farms, in cities, and in deserts. They are known for their cooing, one of the most-recognized bird sounds. It's usually the males who are doing the cooing. Mourning doves can be seen in trees, on the ground, and are often observed sitting on telephone wires. The dove's diet is almost all seeds, but they'll also eat insects or snails. Mourning doves tuck their heads between their shoulders, close to their body, when they sleep.

COLOR: Gray with black spots; pink feet

HEAD: Dark brown or black bill with a short, sharp, curved beak; curved head; black eyes

SHAPE: Medium size; thin tail

RANGE: Across North America

Northern Cardinal
(NOR-thrn KAAR-duh-null)

Northern cardinals are bright red, colorful birds. Cardinals eat a variety of food including seeds, berries, fruits, spiders, and insects. The cardinal's crest on its head and thick, red bills really stand out. Males are known to attack other males invading their territory. Females sing while sitting on their nests, perhaps letting males know when to bring food.

COLOR: Male: bright red with black mask; female: brown with reddish tinge on wings

HEAD: Short, thick, red bill; feathers overlap on back of head

SHAPE: Small to medium size; crest on head

RANGE: Eastern United States; desert Southwest

Northern Flicker
(NOR-thrn FLI-kr)

Northern flickers are in the woodpecker family. They are often seen on the ground finding their favorite foods—ants and termites. Northern flickers do what is called "drumming." They'll pound on wood or metal with their beaks and be as loud as possible. This is to communicate or defend their territory. Both males and females dance as part of their mating ritual, swinging their heads back and forth.

COLOR: Yellow wing flashes; spotted breast, color bands on back, red spot on back of head; males with a black cheek stripe

HEAD: Colorful; long, sharp bill

SHAPE: Medium size

RANGE: Across most of the United States; found in wooded areas

Northern Mockingbird
(NOR-thrn MAA-king-burd)

Northern mockingbirds sing endlessly, sometimes even at night. Males can learn up to 200 songs in their lifetime, with many of their songs in repeat patterns. For a long time, northern mockingbirds were sold in cities, with the best singers getting the highest price. Eventually, the practice of caging wild birds, such as the mockingbird, ended.

COLOR: White underneath; soft gray to black streaks on wings

HEAD: Fairly large; small, black bill

SHAPE: Small to medium size; thin overall; long tail; pointed, slightly curved bill

RANGE: All of the United States except the Pacific Northwest and Northern Plains

Red-Winged Blackbird
(REHD wingd BLAK-burd)

Red-winged blackbirds are found all over North America. Males are glossy black. They also have a bright red patch on their shoulders. Males sit high atop perches, singing while puffing out their shoulders and spreading their wings. Females are mostly brown with streaks of other colors as well. Females stay lower down to the ground, looking for food or building a nest.

COLOR: Male: glossy black with red spot on shoulders; female: mostly brown with yellow tinge on face

HEAD: Round; triangular-shaped bill

SHAPE: Small to medium size; full body; stocky with broad shoulders

RANGE: Across North America

Rock Pigeon
(RAAWK PIH-juhn)

Rock pigeons are seen in cities around the world and were brought to North America in the 1600s. They often live off discarded food and people like to feed them. Rock pigeons drink water through their bills, using them like straws. Rock pigeons nest on building ledges, in barns, under bridges, and on cliffs. When sensing danger, rock pigeons puff their chests, coo, and bow repeatedly.

COLOR: Colors commonly include a gray back, two black bars on the wing, a blue-gray head with a greenish tinting on the neck area; dark area at tip of tail

HEAD: Small; thin, straight bill

SHAPE: Medium size; plump and round body; short legs

RANGE: Across the United States

Ruby-Throated Hummingbird
(ROO-bee THROW-ted HUH-ming-burd)

The ruby-throated hummingbird is an expert flyer. It can hover in one spot and adjust position in the air—forward, backward, up, and down. The ruby-throated hummingbird beats its wings about 53 times per second. In the fall, they migrate to Central America, crossing the Gulf of Mexico in one long flight! Males are known for their bright red throats.

COLOR: Male: red throat, black mask on face, green crown; female: white below and greenish-tinted upper parts

HEAD: Oval- to flat-shaped; long, sharp bill

SHAPE: Tiny size; long wings and tail for the bird's size

RANGE: Eastern half of the United States including the Great Plains

Tufted Titmouse
(TUHF-tehd TIT-mows)

The tufted titmouse is a small bird with a large voice. It has an alarm call that warns others of predators and fades, as if the bird is flying away, while it remains in place. The tufted titmouse cracks open seeds to eat by whacking at them with its sharp bill. It also stores seeds for winter food. Titmice are quite nimble and can be spotted hanging upside down or sideways on trees.

COLOR: Gray above and white below with a peach color wash on its sides, or flanks

HEAD: Large, dark eyes; crest on head; short, sharp bill

SHAPE: Small size; stocky

RANGE: East of the Mississippi River year-round

Song Sparrow
(SAWNG SPEH-roh)

Song sparrows are known for their singing. Males often perch on a branch and sing to attract mates or to defend their territory. Song sparrows search together for nesting spots, but the female builds the nest, often using the same spot each year. They eat a wide variety of food, such as beetles, grasshoppers, spiders, worms, fruits, and berries. There are 31 different kinds of song sparrows—more variety than any other North American bird type.

COLOR: Reddish gray–brown overall; white area down chest; brown to black spots and streaks over most of the rest of the body

HEAD: Flat- to oval-shaped; short, sharp, cone-shaped beak

SHAPE: Small size; puffy round body; long tail

RANGE: Across North America

Steller's Jay
(STEH-lrs JAY)

If you camp out in the mountains out west, you've likely seen the Steller's jay in your campsite. They are noisy birds known to swoop down and steal food. If they find something like a peanut, they'll store it in the crop, or sac, in their throat before flying off. Steller's jays hop around on the ground and often pause to cock their head one way or another as they inspect their surroundings.

COLOR: Front half of bird is black and back half is blue; some color streaks on tail

HEAD: Large; spiky, black crest

SHAPE: Medium size; sharp, strong beak; long tail

RANGE: Western United States; mountainous areas in summer but may move to lower elevations in winter; prefers forested areas

White-Breasted Nuthatch
(WHY-t BREH-sted NUHT-hach)

White-breasted nuthatches are active birds. They are often seen scampering down a tree head first. They get their name, "nuthatch," because they stuff large seeds, like acorns, into trees. Then they whack them with their bill until the seed breaks out. White-breasted nuthatches are small birds with a loud voice—and they sing persistently, which helps birders spot them.

COLOR: Blue-gray back; white cheeks; black cap on head; white belly; red spots near rear

HEAD: Flat to oval shaped; pointed bill

SHAPE: Small size; no neck; short tail

RANGE: Across the United States; found in forests and backyard trees

Yellow Warbler
(YEH-loh WOR-buh-lr)

There are about 50 species of warbler in North America, but the yellow warbler is the most striking due to its bright yellow color. Yellow warblers prefer thickets and wooded areas near streams or wetlands. They can be found near sea level as well as in mountainous areas above 8,000 feet. Warblers are one of North America's most common songbirds.

COLOR: Distinctly yellow with some black streaks on wings and some greenish tinge to backs

HEAD: Round; black eyes

SHAPE: Small, roundish-shaped body; short, thick bill; medium tail length

RANGE: Breeds in North America and Canada, winters in Central and South America

American Kestrel
(uh-MEH-rih-ken KEH-struhl)

The American kestrel is North America's smallest falcon. Kestrels are in the raptor family, meaning they are birds of prey. Kestrels eat insects, birds, rodents, and reptiles. Some kestrels also hunt by **kiting**, where they hover in one spot until prey is seen. Once spotted, the kestrel swoops down and seizes the prey with its feet.

COLOR: Male: rust-colored above with gray-blue wings, black marks across face; female: rust-colored with black slash on face and gray crown

HEAD: Small, round; small, strong, curved bill

SHAPE: Medium size

RANGE: Across North America

Bald Eagle
(bahld EE-gul)

Bald eagles are the national symbol of the United States. They're called "bald" but actually have a white feather-covered head. Bald eagles are often spotted alone; however, many will gather in areas where food is found. Bald eagles eat fish as well as birds, reptiles, small mammals, and **carrion**, or dead animals. When hunting for food, they can dive at speeds up to 100 miles per hour! They build their nests in old growth trees or along rocky areas or cliffs. Their nests can reach up to 6 feet tall.

COLOR: Brown body; white head and tail

HEAD: Large, yellow-gold, hooked-shaped bill

SHAPE: Large size; long wings splayed out; large, strong talons

RANGE: Forested areas near water across the United States

Great Horned Owl
(grate hornd owl)

The great horned owl is known for the tufts, or horns, on its head. These owls use their hooked beak and sharp talons to take down prey. They dine on small animals. The great horned owl is most active at night and can hear sounds up to 10 miles away. Great horned owls cannot move their eyes like people do. Instead they turn their heads side to side.

COLOR: Cinnamon- to gray-colored face

HEAD: Flat; tufts on ears; yellow eyes

SHAPE: Large size; hooked beak; large wings—up to about a 4-foot wingspan

RANGE: Common across the United States in all habitats, including deserts, wetlands, forests, and backyards

Red-Tailed Hawk
(REHD tayld HAAWK)

Red-tailed hawks are the most common hawk on the continent. They are often seen perched on poles and trees near roadsides. Hawks are **carnivores**, or meat-eaters. They'll eat rabbits, squirrels, mice, voles, birds, and even reptiles and snakes. Their broad wings are made for soaring endlessly in the air. Red-tailed hawks can't move their eyes. In order to see to the side, they have to turn their heads.

COLOR: Pale or whitish below, dark brown on top; red tail that is dark at the wing tips and edges of the feathers; brown head with white throat

HEAD: Stout, flat; large, hooked beak

SHAPE: Large size; short, fanned-out red tail; broad wings that splay at the ends

RANGE: Across North America and Canada

Turkey Vulture
(TUR-kee VUHL-chur)

Turkey vultures are often seen eating carrion, or dead animals. They are known for gliding for long stretches at a time, soaring on air currents. They'll also teeter, or tip, their wings when flying. When turkey vultures find a dead animal, several will circle the area and, eventually, land to pull at the meat using their hooked beaks.

COLOR: Black body; red head

HEAD: Wrinkled, featherless red head; pale, hook-shaped beak; black eyes

SHAPE: Large size; long wings splayed out; wings in V shape while flying

RANGE: Almost all of North America, except small parts of the northern Rockies and Great Plains

Great Blue Heron
(grayt bloo HEH-ruhn)

The great blue heron is a large and uniquely shaped bird. They often wade into water and then stay still. When they see something—like a fish—they'll snap it up. If it is a larger fish, the heron will shake it to break the spine before swallowing it. When herons fly, they form their neck into an S-shape. While approaching a landing, they dangle their legs until they reach the ground.

COLOR: Grayish-blue coloring; black crown with plumes

HEAD: Long, sharp orange bill

SHAPE: Large, tall bird; long S-shaped neck; long legs

RANGE: Across the United States; typically near fresh or salt water

Killdeer
(KIL-deer)

Killdeer are shorebirds, but they also live in grassy fields. Often, they run along the ground searching for insects to eat. The killdeer uses a clever method to fool predators called "broken-wing display." It feigns an injured wing, leading a predator away from the nest, then takes off when the predator gets close.

COLOR: Brown on top and white underneath; two black bands across the chest; rust-colored tail

HEAD: Small; long bill; bands of black, white, and brown on head

SHAPE: Small to medium; long and slender; long wings

RANGE: Mexico in winter; southern United States and Pacific coast year-round

Ring-Billed Gull
(RING bild GUHL)

Ring-billed gulls are known for their combination of gray-and-white bodies with yellow, webbed, feet and bills. They also have a distinct black ring around their bill. You'll see them oceanside, but they also live near freshwater lakes. Ring-billed gulls fly up to 40 miles per hour. They'll drop objects in the air and swoop down and catch them.

COLOR: Black band, or ring, on yellow bill; yellow legs; pale-colored eyes, white belly, pale gray back; black end of tail

HEAD: Short, thick bill; tan spotting on head or neck

SHAPE: Medium

RANGE: East and West Coasts, Great Lakes, Great Salt Lake, and rivers; southern United States in winter

American Coot
(uh-MEH-rih-ken KOOT)

Coots are easily identified by their dark body and head, and white bill. They swim using their long toes and lobed, or rounded, feet. In winter, they find water with ducks and other birds, populating thousands of birds in one place. It takes quite a bit of effort for a coot to fly. They start by running on water and frantically beating their wings, finally taking off after they've run 10 to 20 feet.

COLOR: Dark gray overall; white bill with tip of black at the end

HEAD: Small, round; bill slopes downward

SHAPE: Medium size; pointed bill; long toes; plump, round body; skinny legs

RANGE: Seen throughout the United States; breeds in the Northern Plains and Canada

Canada Goose
(KEH-ne-de goos)

Canada geese are often seen in fields, ponds, lakes, and parks. The white strap under their chin is their most identifiable feature. They are often observed flying in V formations. Canada geese forage, or search, for seeds, grasses, or berries to eat. They also dab their heads into the water to grab vegetation. They are nicknamed "the big honker" due to their distinct calls while flying.

COLOR: Brown on top, white underneath; white stripe or strap under chin

HEAD: Oval to round shape; wide, oval, black-colored beak

SHAPE: Large size; oval-shaped body; long, curved neck

RANGE: Migratory, breeding in the northern United States, Canada, and Arctic in summer; living in most of United States in winter

Double-Crested Cormorant
(DUH-bl KREH-stehd KOR-mr-ant)

The double-crested cormorant looks slightly prehistoric, reminding people of dinosaurs. They are often seen standing on docks, piers, or in rocky areas. They spread their wings to dry after fishing. Cormorant feathers are not very waterproof. This allows them to swim low in the water and sink a bit, as well as dive more easily to catch fish.

COLOR: Orange to yellow skin near bill and chin

HEAD: Small tufts on the side of the head, if breeding; bill same size as head

SHAPE: Large; long tail, twisted neck, hook-shaped bill

RANGE: Across the United States when breeding; in Florida year-round

Mallard
(MA-lrd)

Mallards are what most people know as ducks. They are found in wetland habitats including marshes, ponds, rivers, lakes, and **estuaries**, or the places where a river meets the ocean. They are known for unique behaviors including head bobbing, threatening an intruder with an open bill, or pushing against each other chest to chest. Their distinct quack is made only by the females.

COLOR: Male: dark green head; body a mix of gray, brown, and black with a blue patch on wings; female: mottled, or speckled, brown all over

HEAD: Round; flat, wide bill

SHAPE: Large, long, powerful body; short tail

RANGE: Common across the United States

Field Guide:
Backyard Birds
and Beyond

American Dipper
(uh-MEH-rih-ken DIH-pr)

American dippers are seen near streams with rushing, unpolluted water. Dippers are chunky, round, mostly grayish-brown birds with small tails. They have thin, mostly dark, long bills. The American dipper is North America's only aquatic songbird. They are sometimes seen near rushing water, bobbing up and down.

COLOR: Shades of grayish brown

HEAD: Thick neck; long, thin bill

SHAPE: Medium size

RANGE: Mountainous areas of the west

American Pipit
(uh-MEH-rih-ken PIH-puht)

American pipits are migrating songbirds. Pipits are small birds with sharply pointed bills. They are mostly mixed or streaky gray above; with some yellow to gray to cinnamon beneath. Pipits have an extra-long hind toe. This likely helps them walk more easily on rough ground and snow.

COLOR: Mixed gray and streaky above; gray to white to yellow underneath

HEAD: Small, round

SHAPE: Small size

RANGE: Alpine areas in summer; winter in warmer areas of the United States

American Tree Sparrow
(uh-MEH-rih-ken TREE SPEH-roh)

American tree sparrows are songbirds. They fluff out their feathers, making them appear chubby. This traps air underneath and keeps them warm. A tree sparrow can be identified by the rust-colored cap on its head and at the back of its eyes. American tree sparrows have to eat and drink 30 percent of their body weight each day to survive.

COLOR: Combination of brown, gray, reddish, and white; rust-colored at head cap and back of eyes

HEAD: Small

SHAPE: Small size

RANGE: Across most of the United States

Anna's Hummingbird
(AA-nuhz HUH-ming-burd)

Anna's hummingbirds grace the West Coast and parts of the desert Southwest. The male's head and throat are rainbow-like rosy-red to pink. Females are metallic green above and grayish below. Anna's hummingbirds are about the size of a Ping-Pong ball and weigh about as much as a nickel.

COLOR: Male: rosy-red to pink, orange or brown over throat and head; female: metallic green above, gray below

HEAD: Ultra-long, straight bill

SHAPE: Tiny size

RANGE: West Coast and desert Southwest

Belted Kingfisher
(BEL-tuhd KING-fih-shr)

Belted kingfishers are striking-looking birds seen near shorelines. They dive at fish and crawdads, pinch them with their bills, and fly back and swallow the prey whole. Both males and females are blue-gray, though females have a chestnut-colored band on their bellies. Males have a distinct head crest.

COLOR: Blue-gray overall; female: chestnut area on belly

HEAD: Long, dagger-like bill; male: crest on head

SHAPE: Small to medium size

RANGE: Across the United States

Bewick's Wren
(BEW-iks REN)

Bewick's wren is an active songbird. It is a small bird with an extra-long tail, usually held upright. Bewick's wrens are brown and gray with a white stripe over the eye. They are known to have a wide range of vocalizations, including whistles, soft sounds, and a whirring or ringing tone.

COLOR: Brown to gray above, lighter underneath; long, banded tail with white spots

HEAD: White eyeline above eye

SHAPE: Small size

RANGE: Western states, expanding into Texas

Black-Billed Magpie
(BLAK bild MAG-pie)

Black-billed magpies are medium-size birds with long tails. They appear almost all black and white. If seen up close and in good light, some magpies have a blue-green sheen to them. Magpies are sometimes seen perched on large animals, such as deer and moose, picking off ticks to eat.

COLOR: Mixture of black and white with some blue-green sheen

HEAD: Short, thick bill

SHAPE: Medium size

RANGE: Western United States and Northern Plains

Black-Chinned Hummingbird
(BLAK chind HUH-ming-burd)

Black-chinned hummingbirds live in diverse terrain. They can be found in deserts, mountains, and even along the Gulf Coast in Texas. Males have the namesake black chin with an area of iridescent purple next to it. The female's throat is pale. While resting, their hearts beat 480 times per minute!

COLOR: Metallic green above and gray-white below; male: black chin with purple base; female: pale throated

HEAD: Long, straight black bill

SHAPE: Small size; slender build

RANGE: Western United States

Black Tern
(blak turn)

Black terns live near marshes in summer. In winter, they migrate to tropical coasts. Black terns are a mix of charcoal gray and black. They have a thick black bill. When not breeding, they feed off fish in tropical oceans. Terns live in colonies with, sometimes, thousands of birds.

COLOR: Charcoal gray and black mix, some white underneath

HEAD: Black

SHAPE: Medium size

RANGE: Wetlands and coastal areas across much of the United States

Blue-Gray Gnatcatcher
(bloo gray NAT-keh-chr)

Blue-gray gnatcatchers are tiny songbirds. Though small, they have long legs and a long tail. Males are blue-gray above and white below. Females are gray above. As the world's climate continues to warm, blue-gray gnatcatchers have extended their habitat about 200 miles farther north.

COLOR: Male: blue above and white below; female: mostly gray

HEAD: Gray; male: black V on forehead

SHAPE: Small size

RANGE: Southern two-thirds of the United States

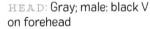

Bobolink
(BAA-buh-luhngk)

Bobolinks are striking songbirds. Males have a mixture of black and white on their bodies, with golden yellow on the back of the head and neck. Females are streaky brown. The bobolink migrates to South America, and over its life, it may travel a mileage equaling four to five trips around the world.

COLOR: Male: black and white with yellow patch on back of head and neck; female: streaky brown

HEAD: Flat

SHAPE: Small to medium size

RANGE: Eastern United States, Northern Plains, and Rocky Mountains

Brewer's Blackbird
(BROO-urz BLAK-burd)

Brewer's blackbirds are stunning. Males are inky black, but with a dark blue-green sheen on their head and body. Females are mostly brown. Brewer's blackbirds' eggs have a variety of color and patterns. This helps them stay camouflaged and safe. They live across most of the United States.

COLOR: Male: inky black with a dark green to blue sheen on back of head and neck; female: brown

HEAD: Round

SHAPE: Medium size

RANGE: Across the United States, except the Northeast

Brown Creeper
(brown KREE-pr)

Brown creepers are tiny songbirds that prefer living in large trees. They are mixed brown above and white beneath. Brown creepers have a long, slightly downward-curved bill. They also have a long tail. Brown creepers build nests that resemble hammocks in parts of trees.

COLOR: Mottled or mixed brown above, white beneath

HEAD: Long, thin bill; no neck

SHAPE: Tiny size; long tail

RANGE: Across the United States

Brown Thrasher
(brown THRA-shr)

Brown thrashers are attractive songbirds that can be seen east of the Rocky Mountains. Thrashers have long body parts—tail, legs, and bill. They are reddish brown above and mostly white below. They are known for their large repertoire of songs—more than any other songbird in the United States!

COLOR: Brown above, streaked whitish below

HEAD: Yellow eyes; long, downward-curved bill

SHAPE: Medium size

RANGE: East of the Rocky Mountains

Cassin's Finch

(KAS-sinz FINCH)

Cassin's finch is a small, rose-tinged finch. It can be identified by its peaked head and straight bill. Males have a red, peaked crown and are mostly pale underneath. Females are streaked brown and white. The red color of the male's crown comes from the food it eats.

COLOR: Male: red crown, pale underneath; female: streaked brown

HEAD: Peaked

SHAPE: Small size

RANGE: Mountain regions of the western United States

Chimney Swift

(CHIM-nee swift)

Chimney swifts maneuver swiftly around objects to catch insects. Chimney swifts are a dark gray–brown color with a pale throat. They have a long, tube-shaped body and curved wings. Their long claws don't allow them to perch. Instead, they cling sideways to chimney walls and other vertical surfaces. They got their name from their fondness for building nests in chimneys!

COLOR: Gray-brown overall with a pale throat

HEAD: Flat; no neck

SHAPE: Small to medium size

RANGE: Eastern half of the United States

Chipping Sparrow
(CHIH-ping SPEH-roh)

Chipping sparrows are songbirds commonly seen across the United States. They are small, with a slender build and long tail. Adults are identified by their rust-colored crown and black eyeline. Chipping sparrows will eat many kinds of birdseed, so they are often seen at backyard feeders.

COLOR: Frosty gray underneath; rusty-crowned above

HEAD: Rusty crown; black eyeline

SHAPE: Small size

RANGE: Across the United States

Clark's Nutcracker
(klaarks NUHT-kra-kr)

Clark's nutcrackers live in mountainous areas of the west. They are a stark, beautiful contrast in colors, with a soft-gray body and black-and-white wings and tail fan. Nutcrackers tear into pine cones for seeds. They store the seeds in summer and remember each location in winter so they can feed.

COLOR: Soft gray, white, and black

HEAD: Long, sharp bill; white around the eyes

SHAPE: Small to medium size

RANGE: Mountainous areas of the western United States

Cliff Swallow
(KLIF SWAA-loh)

Cliff swallows are small birds known for building mud nests. Cliff swallows have a small head and square-shaped tail. They have a dark blue back and a reddish or rust-colored face with a white patch on the forehead. Cliff swallows nest in colonies, sometimes with thousands of other birds.

COLOR: Dark blue back; rust-colored face

HEAD: Small; small, sharp bill; white patch on forehead

SHAPE: Small size; compact

RANGE: Across the United States

Eastern Bluebird
(EE-strn BLOO-burd)

Eastern bluebirds live east of the Rocky Mountains. Males are a striking, deep blue above and rust-colored on their throat and breast. Females are gray above with blue-tinted wings and orange-brown beneath. Though they eat mostly insects, eastern bluebirds will sometimes devour frogs, lizards, and even snakes.

COLOR: Male: blue above and rusty beneath; female: grayish above with blue-tinted wings

HEAD: Large

SHAPE: Small size

RANGE: East of the Rocky Mountains

Eastern Kingbird
(EE-strn KING-burd)

Eastern kingbirds can be seen from the Rocky Mountains to the East Coast. Eastern kingbirds are broad-shouldered and typically perch in an upright position. They look dignified with their black-and-white plumage. Eastern kingbirds will take on and harass much larger birds who encroach into their territory.

COLOR: Black above and white below; white tip on tail
HEAD: Large, dark; short, straight bill
SHAPE: Small to medium size
RANGE: From the Rocky Mountains to the East Coast

Eastern Phoebe
(EE-strn FEE-bee)

Eastern phoebes are plump songbirds that live in wooded areas. Phoebes are active birds, flying about in search of insects. They're grayish to brown above and white below. In 1804, an Eastern phoebe became the first banded bird in North America. This was done to track the path of its migration.

COLOR: Gray to brown above, white below
HEAD: Large, darker colored
SHAPE: Small size; plump
RANGE: East of the Rocky Mountains

Fox Sparrow
(FAAKS SPEH-roh)

Fox sparrows are songbirds named for their rich, red, "fox-like" coloring. They are typically reddish brown overall, though lighter underneath. Fox sparrows along the Pacific coast are usually much darker in color. Fox sparrows have been spotted in remote areas such as Greenland and Iceland—likely traveling there by ship.

COLOR: Fox-like, rusty coloring above; lighter below

HEAD: Rusty- to gray-colored

SHAPE: Small size

RANGE: Forested areas across the United States

Gray Catbird
(gray KAT-burd)

Gray catbirds are found in open, wooded areas. They have a long, rounded-off tail, long legs, and a straight bill. Catbirds are gray with a dark cap on their heads. They may have a small amount of cinnamon color underneath. Gray catbird songs may last up to 10 minutes!

COLOR: Gray overall

HEAD: Black cap

SHAPE: Medium size; lean or thin appearance

RANGE: From the Rocky Mountains to the East Coast

Great Crested Flycatcher
(grayt KREH-stehd FLY-keh-chr)

Great crested flycatchers are a pleasing-to-look-at blend of lemon yellow underneath, with a reddish to gray head and olive-colored backs. They are up to eight inches long with broad shoulders and a large head. Great crested flycatchers are known to use snakeskin in their nests.

COLOR: Lemon yellow underneath; reddish tail; gray- to olive-colored above

HEAD: Large, peaked

SHAPE: Large for a flycatcher

RANGE: East of the Rocky Mountains

Greater Prairie Chicken
(GRAY-tr PREH-ree CHI-kn)

Greater prairie chickens are mottled or mixed brown, black, and white. When courting, males raise the feathers on their neck, exposing orange air sacs that they fill with air to create a booming noise. All of this is done while drumming their feet and making cackling and whooping sounds.

COLOR: Mix of brown, white, and black

HEAD: Round; small neck and bill

SHAPE: Medium to large size

RANGE: Grasslands of the Great Plains in the United States

Greater Roadrunner
(GRAY-tr ROHD-ruh-nr)

Greater roadrunners are large, uniquely shaped landbirds. Roadrunners are mostly a streaky brown color, but lighter underneath. They can be up to two feet long from bill to tail—and they run fast, up to 20 miles per hour! This makes them the fastest landbird or runner in North America.

COLOR: Streaky brown overall

HEAD: Long, straight bill; crest on head

SHAPE: Tall; long, thin legs, tail, body, and neck

RANGE: Desert Southwest of the United States

Hairy Woodpecker
(HEH-ree WUHD-peh-kr)

Hairy woodpeckers are easily identified by their black-and-white body and long bill. Males also have a red patch on the back of the head. Hairy woodpeckers will sometimes follow pileated woodpeckers (see page 80) to their feeding hole looking for food. Once abandoned, hairy woodpeckers take over and eat any insects that were missed.

COLOR: Black-and-white overall; male: red patch at back of head

HEAD: Square

SHAPE: Small to medium size

RANGE: Forested areas of the United States

Hermit Thrush
(HUR-muht thruhsh)

Hermit thrushes are found in forested areas, open fields, and in dense thickets. They are chunky shaped and their bill tilts upward. Hermit thrushes are brown above with a red tail and white underneath with brown spots. They'll shake bits of grass with their feet to get the insects out to make it easier to find and eat them.

COLOR: Brown above; reddish tail; white below with brown spotting

HEAD: Round

SHAPE: Small to medium size

RANGE: Across the United States

Horned Lark
(hornd LAARK)

Horned larks are unique-looking songbirds. They stand out thanks to the combined striped yellow face, black mask, and tiny horns on their head. Horned larks are brown above and whitish below. They can live at sea level and all the way up to a 13,000-foot elevation.

COLOR: Brown with white underneath; male: black mask

HEAD: Small, round; male: tiny horns on head

SHAPE: Small size

RANGE: Most of the United States over winter

Indigo Bunting
(IN-duh-go BUHN-ting)

Indigo buntings are striking songbirds. Males are a sky-blue color. Females are mostly brown with a light-colored throat. Nicknamed "blue canaries," they are known for singing from dawn to dusk. Indigo buntings migrate at night, flying more than 1,200 miles to South America using the stars as their guide.

COLOR: Male: mostly sky blue; female: brownish overall

HEAD: Male: blue; female: brownish

SHAPE: Small size

RANGE: East of the Rocky Mountains

Lesser Goldfinch
(LEH-sr GOHLD-finch)

Lesser goldfinches are tiny songbirds. Males stand out due to their bright yellow color contrasting with a black back with white patches. Females are olive-colored on their back and yellow underneath. Lesser goldfinches usually build their nests four to eight feet off the ground, hidden by leaves.

COLOR: Male: bright yellow with black back and white patches; female: olive-green back, yellow underneath

HEAD: Glassy black color

SHAPE: Tiny size

RANGE: Western United States

Loggerhead Shrike
(LAA-gr-hed SHRAIK)

Loggerhead shrikes are songbirds. They have a gray head and back of neck, and black wings. The shrike also has a black mask that goes from its bill back to its neck. Loggerhead shrikes impale insects on a thorn or piece of barbed wire so they are easier to eat.

COLOR: Gray with black mask and wings; white spots on tail and wings

HEAD: Large; thick, hooked bill

SHAPE: Small to medium size

RANGE: Most of the United States

Northern Bobwhite
(NOR-thrn BAHB-whyt)

Northern bobwhites are part of the quail family. They are heard more than seen due to their whistle-like call. Bobwhites sport a colorful palette, with a round body, small head, and short tail. Bobwhites prefer to be in small groups with other birds, foraging on the ground for food.

COLOR: Mix of brown, reddish brown, gray, white, and black

HEAD: Small

SHAPE: Medium size

RANGE: Fields and grasses in the eastern United States

Northern Oriole
(NOR-thrn OR-ee-uhl)

Northern orioles are colorful songbirds that can be seen east of the Rocky Mountains. Males are easily identified by their bright orange feathers. Orioles feed by stabbing fruit with a closed bill, then opening their mouths and drinking the juice. The oriole's sweet song is often a sign of spring.

COLOR: Male: orange tail feathers, rump, and under-neath; female: yellow to brown

HEAD: Male: black head; female: brown to yellow head

SHAPE: Small to medium size

RANGE: Eastern United States

Orange-Crowned Warbler
(AW-ruhnj krownd WOR-buh-lr)

The orange crown of the orange-crowned warbler is rarely seen. Only when excited or agitated will the bird raise its head feathers, showing the color. Orange-crowned warblers are yellow to olive with some gray overall, with short wings and a short tail. They usually build their nests on the ground.

COLOR: Yellow to olive to light gray overall

HEAD: Little neck; large eyes

SHAPE: Small size

RANGE: Across the United States

Pileated Woodpecker
(PIE-lee-ay-tid WUHD-peh-kr)

The pileated woodpecker is a very large woodpecker, some 16 to 19 inches in length. It is mainly black with white striping across its face and a red crest on its head. Males also have a red cheek stripe. Pileated woodpeckers whack at dead or downed trees to get to ants for food.

COLOR: Black-and-white stripes on face and neck; male: red cheek stripe

HEAD: Triangular shape

SHAPE: Medium to large size

RANGE: Eastern half of the United States, Pacific Northwest, and California's Sierra Nevada Mountains

Pine Siskin
(PIE-n SIH-skn)

Pine siskins are **nomadic** songbirds, moving from place to place in search of food. They are known for their short, sharp, pointed bills; short, notched tails; and brown coloring with bits of yellow on the wings and tail. Pine siskins store seeds in a part of their esophagus called a *crop*.

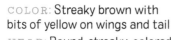

COLOR: Streaky brown with bits of yellow on wings and tail

HEAD: Round, streaky-colored

SHAPE: Small size

RANGE: Across the United States

Purple Finch
(PUR-pl FINCH)

Purple finches have been described as a "sparrow dipped in raspberry juice." The males have the raspberry-colored head, back, and neck. Females are streaky brown. Both have some white underneath. Purple finches are known to copy sounds from several other types of birds.

COLOR: Male: raspberry-colored head, back, and neck; female: streaky brown

HEAD: Strong, cone-shaped bill

SHAPE: Small size; chunky

RANGE: East of the Rocky Mountains and West Coast

Purple Martin
(PUR-pl MAR-tin)

Purple martins are in the swallow family. Males are dark purple overall but with brown and black on their wings and tails. Females are duller in color and have a gray collar around their neck. Purple martins drink water by skimming along a pond and scooping up the water with their bills.

COLOR: Male: dark purple with brown and black on wings and tail; female: duller

HEAD: Small; slightly hooked bill

SHAPE: Small size

RANGE: From the Rocky Mountains to the east; along the Pacific coast and parts of the Southwest

Raven
(RAY-vuhn)

Ravens are highly intelligent, medium- to large-size birds. Black like crows, but much larger, ravens have a thick, shaggy neck, heavy bill, and long tail. Ravens, historically, have followed people—whether hunters or pioneers. They learned that where there are people, there will be food.

COLOR: All black
HEAD: Heavy, curved bill; shaggy feathers at neck
SHAPE: Medium to large size
RANGE: Western United States

Red-Naped Sapsucker
(REHD-naypd SAP-suh-kr)

Red-naped sapsuckers are woodpeckers. Both males and females are a black-and-white mixture with a red throat and crown. They are known to be around if rows of holes are seen in tree trunks. These are where sapsuckers drill trying to get to the sugar sap in the tree.

COLOR: Black and white with red throat
HEAD: Strong, sharply pointed bill; red cap on head and neck
SHAPE: Medium size
RANGE: Western United States

Ring-Necked Pheasant
(RING nekt FEH-znt)

Ring-necked pheasants are chicken-shaped birds with especially long tails. Males have a bright red face, greenish-blue neck, and a white ring around the collar. Females are brown overall with black spotting. Strong muscles allow ring-necked pheasants to fly fast, reaching speeds of 40 miles per hour.

COLOR: Male: red face, green-blue neck; female: brown with black spots

HEAD: Males have colorful heads

SHAPE: Large size

RANGE: Across the United States

Rose-Breasted Grosbeak
(ROZE BREH-stuhd GROWS-beek)

The rose-breasted grosbeak is a medium-size songbird. Males are black with white spots on top and white underneath, with a bright, rosy chest. Females are a streaky mixed brown with a white line above the eye. They have large, thick, triangular-shaped bills. Rose-breasted grosbeaks have an especially sweet song.

COLOR: Male: mix of black, white, and rosy chest area; female: brown and streaky

HEAD: Large, thick, triangular-shaped bills; male: black head; female: streaky brown

SHAPE: Medium size

RANGE: Eastern United States

Ruby-Crowned Kinglet
(ROO-bee krownd KING-luht)

The ruby-crowned kinglet is a tiny songbird. Kinglets have large heads, no necks, and a tiny tail and bill. They are olive green overall. Adult males have a bright red crown that shows only when they are excited or agitated. Ruby-crowned kinglets lay up to 12 eggs in a nest.

COLOR: Olive green overall; white around eyes and wings

HEAD: Large and flattish; male: bright red crown

SHAPE: Tiny size

RANGE: Higher elevations north in summer; lower elevations in south in winter

Ruffed Grouse
(ruhft growz)

Ruffed grouses are highly camouflaged and are often heard before they are seen. They make a unique sound described as like an engine trying to start. Grouses are plump birds with a crest on their heads and dark chocolate–brown to black neck feathers, called a "ruff," which is where they get their name. In winter, the ruffed grouse grows projections on its toes to help it walk through snow.

COLOR: Spotted mix of red, gray, brown, and white

HEAD: Crest on head; black eyes; short bill

SHAPE: Medium size

RANGE: Northern parts of the United States and the mountains

Rufous Hummingbird
(ROO-fuhs HUH-ming-burd)

Rufous hummingbirds migrate from Alaska and Canada to Mexico. Males have an orange back and belly and red throat. Females are green above with some orange on their throats. Both have long, straight bills that they use mostly to eat nectar from colorful flowers, but at times they will eat insects for protein and fat. Their 4,000-mile migration is one of the longest of any bird in the world.

COLOR: Male: orange at back and belly; red throat; female: green above with some orange at the throat

HEAD: Thick neck and long, thin bill

SHAPE: Tiny

RANGE: Western United States

Say's Phoebe
(SAYZ FEE-bee)

Say's phoebes are plump songbirds. They pump or bob their tails while perched, and they often nest on buildings. Say's phoebes are grayish to brown above, with a cinnamon-colored belly. They have a large nesting range, from central Mexico all the way to the Arctic.

COLOR: Grayish to brown above; cinnamon belly

HEAD: Large; flat top

SHAPE: Small to medium size

RANGE: Western United States

Scarlet Tanager
(SKAAR-luht TAN-uh-jr)

Scarlet tanagers migrate to eastern parts of North America in summer. Tanagers stay high in trees and are often heard before seen. Males have bright red bodies with slick, black wings. Females are light yellow with grayish wings. Female scarlet tanagers sing to males while gathering materials for their nest.

COLOR: Male: red bodies with black wings; female: light yellow with gray wings

HEAD: Large

SHAPE: Small to medium size

RANGE: Migrate between the eastern half of North America in summer and South America in winter

Snow Bunting
(snoh BUHN-ting)

Snow buntings live on the ground. Males are mostly snowy white with a black back. Females have a streaky, mixed-color back and are white underneath. Snow buntings have short, cone-shaped bills. They breed in the Arctic, migrating south in winter, and returning to the Arctic in summer. To keep the nest warm, males bring food about every 15 minutes to the sitting female.

COLOR: Male: white with black back; female: mixed-colored back, white underneath

HEAD: Round, white

SHAPE: Small to medium size

RANGE: All areas of the United States except the south

Spotted Towhee
(SPAA-tuhd TAW-hee)

Spotted towhees are striking birds that live in and among thickets. Males are black on their upper body and throat, with wings and back spotted white. Females are gray to brown where the males are black. Spotted towhees hop and scratch backward on the ground, helping them uncover food.

COLOR: Male: black upper body with white spots; female: brown where males are black

HEAD: Thick, pointed bill; thick, short neck

SHAPE: Small to medium size

RANGE: Western two-thirds of the United States

Swainson's Thrush
(SWAYN-suhns thruhsh)

Swainson's thrush is a small, thin songbird. It has medium-length wings and a tail. Swainson's thrush is brown above and white underneath, with a spotted belly. It is sometimes hard to know where their song is coming from. Is the bird moving around, or is the song bouncing off trees?

COLOR: Brown above, white below; spotted throat and chest

HEAD: Round; short, straight bill

SHAPE: Small size

RANGE: Across the United States

Veery
(VEER-ee)

Veeries are small songbirds known for their "veer" sound while singing. Veeries have plump bodies and a long tail. They are cinnamon brown above with a white, spotted belly area below. Veeries can migrate up to 160 miles in one night, flying more than one mile high.

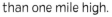

COLOR: Cinnamon brown above; white with brown spotting below

HEAD: Round; black eyes

SHAPE: Small to medium size

RANGE: Eastern two-thirds of the United States

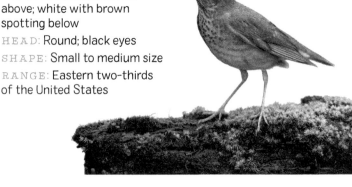

Warbling Vireo
(WOR-buh-luhng VEE-ree-oh)

Warbling vireos are songbirds. They stay high in trees, looking for caterpillars to eat. They are gray- to olive-colored above and white below, with some yellow on the sides. Warbling vireos sometimes raise the chicks of brown-headed cowbirds who have laid eggs in the vireo's nest.

COLOR: Gray- to olive-colored above; white below; yellow on sides

HEAD: Round; thick, straight bill

SHAPE: Small size; chunky-shaped body

RANGE: Across the United States

Western Meadowlark
(WEH-strn MEH-doh-laark)

Western meadowlarks are medium-size songbirds. They have a flat head and long, thin bill. Breeding adults have a distinct yellow chest. Meadowlarks feed by forcing their strong bill into the ground and prying it open. This process, called **gaping**, provides access to insects underground for food.

COLOR: Brown, black, and buff upper parts with a distinct yellow belly

HEAD: Flat, with a long, thin bill

SHAPE: Small to medium size

RANGE: Western two-thirds of the United States

Western Tanager
(WEH-strn TAN-uh-jr)

Western tanagers are brilliantly colored songbirds seen from the Great Plains to the Pacific coast. Their orange to red head, yellow body, and black wings and tail make for quite a sight. The redness in the western tanager's feathers most likely comes from some of the insects they eat.

COLOR: Orange to red head, yellow body

HEAD: Colored; thick, cone-shaped bill

SHAPE: Small size; long tail

RANGE: Western half of the United States

Western Wood-Pewee
(WEH-strn wuhd PEE-wee)

Western wood-pewees are flycatchers that return to the wooded areas of the western United States in summer. When they do, the forests are alive with their "pewee"-like call. Western wood-pewees are gray to brown overall, though lighter underneath. They migrate to South America in winter.

COLOR: Gray to brown overall, lighter underneath

HEAD: Peaked crown; short, sharp bill

SHAPE: Small size

RANGE: Western United States

White-Crowned Sparrow
(WHY-t krownd SPEH-roh)

White-crowned sparrows spend their winters in North America. White-crowned sparrows are known for the distinctive black and white stripes across their heads. They are small birds with a long tail. White-crowned sparrows can migrate up to 300 miles in just one night!

COLOR: Streaky gray, brown overall

HEAD: Black-and-white stripes; peak shape at head

SHAPE: Small size; long tail

RANGE: Across the United States in winter; western states year-round

Wild Turkey
(WHY-ld TUR-kee)

There is nothing quite like spotting a wild turkey. Males are known for their red-and-blue heads and fanned-out tail. Females are brown overall. Wild turkeys also have a large, plump body and a long neck and legs. Wild turkey fossils have been dated up to five million years old.

COLOR: Male: red and blue heads; female: brown

HEAD: Round; **wattle**, or area of skin that ranges in color from red to gray to dull (depending on their mood), hangs down from the male's colorful face

SHAPE: Very large size

RANGE: Across much of the United States.

Yellow-Bellied Sapsucker
(YEH-loh BEH-leed SAP-suh-kr)

Yellow-bellied sapsuckers are part of the woodpecker family. They have black-and-white-patterned bodies with red throats and foreheads. They are small for a woodpecker, with heavy, sharp bills. Sapsuckers poke holes into trees to lap up sap and any insects trapped inside using their brush-tipped tongues.

COLOR: Black-and-white bodies; red throat and forehead; yellowish belly

HEAD: Red forehead; sharp, strong bill

SHAPE: Medium size

RANGE: Eastern half of the United States

Yellow–Billed Cuckoo
(YEH-loh bild KOO-koo)

Yellow-billed cuckoos are slim and long, with a long tail and long, yellow bill. Their posture makes them appear hunched over. Yellow-billed cuckoos also have large white spots on their black tail. They eat caterpillars and can devour up to 100 at a time!

COLOR: Light brown above and white below; white-and-black mix on tail

HEAD: Flat; bill almost as long as the head

SHAPE: Medium size

RANGE: Eastern half of the United States

Yellow–Rumped Warbler
(YEH-loh RUHMPT WOR-buh-lr)

Yellow-rumped warblers are beautiful songbirds seen across the United States. Males and females are gray overall but white on their wings, with areas of yellow on their faces, sides, and rump. Yellow-rumped warblers join with other warblers to make flocks sometimes numbering in the thousands.

COLOR: Gray with some white on wings; yellow at face, sides, and rump

HEAD: Black mask with white or yellow throat

SHAPE: Small size

RANGE: Across the United States

Yellow-Throated Vireo
(YEH-loh THROW-ted VEE-ree-oh)

Yellow-throated vireos are small songbirds. They are known for their bright yellow throat area and what looks like yellow circles around their eyes. Yellow-throated vireos have olive-green heads and white marks on their wings. Males take turns with females incubating their eggs and taking care of their chicks.

COLOR: Yellow throat and yellow circles around the eyes; olive-green head

HEAD: Large; thick bill

SHAPE: Small size; chunky shape

RANGE: Great Plains to the East Coast

Barn Owl
(baarn owl)

Barn owls are medium-size raptors that prowl at night—silently. Barn owls have a flat, round, pale face and are pale underneath. Their wings are spotted gray-brown. Barn owls swallow their prey whole, then spit up the undigestible remains in a lump of fur and bones called a pellet.

COLOR: White face; brown, spotted wings and body

HEAD: Roundish; heart-shaped

SHAPE: Medium to large size

RANGE: Across the United States, except parts of the far north

Burrowing Owl
(BURR-oh-ing OWL)

Burrowing owls are found in the western United States. Burrowing owls are brown- to sandy-colored with bright yellow eyes. They live in underground burrows that they dig or take over from other animals. Burrowing owls lay animal dung at their underground entrance to attract beetles and other insects to eat.

COLOR: Mottled or spotted to mixed brown and white
HEAD: Large; yellow bill
SHAPE: Small size for an owl; long legs
RANGE: Western half of the United States

California Condor
(ka-luh-FORN-yuh KAWN-dor)

California condors are North America's largest landbird. Once almost extinct, condors are now recovering and are expanding their range. The California condor has a featherless, pink head and thick bill. Condors soar on air currents. While doing so, their fingered wings are clearly seen, as are the white patches under their wings.

COLOR: Black on top; white patches under the wings
HEAD: Featherless, pink
SHAPE: Up to a 10-foot wing span; ends of wings splay out
RANGE: Parts of California, Utah, Arizona, and Nevada

Common Nighthawk
(KAA-muhn NITE-haawk)

Often heard before seen, the common nighthawk roams the skies at dawn and dusk across most of the United States. They are slender birds with long wings and tails. Common nighthawks are a combination of gray, light brown, white, and black. Unlike most raptors, the nighthawk's diet consists mostly of flying insects.

COLOR: Gray, light brown, black, and white; white patch on wings

HEAD: Large eyes; short neck

SHAPE: Medium size

RANGE: United States, except parts of California, Arizona, and Nevada

Cooper's Hawk
(KOO-prz haawk)

Cooper's hawks are raptors seen across the United States. They have a blue-gray body, a dark spot on top of their head, and red eyes. Great hunters, Cooper's hawks fly in and around trees looking for birds to eat. They catch birds with their feet and kill them by squeezing.

COLOR: Blue-gray body on top; white to reddish underneath

HEAD: Large; flat with dark cap; red eyes

SHAPE: Medium to large size

RANGE: Across the United States

Eastern Screech Owl
(EE-strn skreeech owl)

Eastern screech owls are small for owls. They are heard more often than seen. Screech owls can be either reddish or gray overall, but with streaky layers of coloring. They also have large heads and pointed ear tufts. Males are smaller than females and are more agile hunters.

COLOR: Mostly grayish or reddish with streaky coloring

HEAD: Large; little or no neck

SHAPE: Medium size

RANGE: Eastern United States

Golden Eagle
(GOHLD-un EE-gul)

Golden eagles are large, powerful raptors. They are dark brown with long wings that splay out at the ends. They have a golden nape, or back of the neck. Golden eagles are great hunters. They prefer small animals as food, but can actually take down large animals such as livestock, swooping down unexpectedly and using their very strong talons to attack.

COLOR: Dark brown with golden back of the neck

HEAD: Large; sharp, brown, curved bill meant for tearing into meat

SHAPE: Very large

RANGE: Across the United States

King Rail
(king rayl)

The king rail is a medium-size waterbird. They have chicken-like features, including a plump belly and long, strong legs and feet. The king rail is well camouflaged with stripes and spots of brown coloring to keep it safe from predators such as foxes and coyotes. If the king rail finds food on land, it will dunk it in water before eating it.

COLOR: Striped mixture of brown, with spots of black and white

HEAD: Flattish; long bill

SHAPE: Medium size

RANGE: Atlantic Coast and Gulf of Mexico

Merlin
(MR-luhn)

Merlins are falcons that live in open forests and grasslands. They have stocky builds, broad chests, and pointed wings. Males are dark gray overall and may have a bluish tint, with a thin white eyebrow. Females are larger than males and mostly brown. Merlins don't build their own nests. Instead, they take over the old nests of other raptors or crows.

COLOR: Male: dark gray overall; female: brown

HEAD: Large, bulky

SHAPE: Medium size; stocky, strong build

RANGE: Across the United States

Mississippi Kite
(MIH-suh-si-pee KIE-t)

Mississippi kites are raptors. They are a mix of gray to black on their bodies and gray to white on their heads. Kites build their nests next to or near wasps' nests, likely to protect chicks against predators. They travel all the way to South America for winter.

COLOR: Gray to black body
HEAD: Large, mostly white
SHAPE: Medium to large size
RANGE: Southeastern United States and areas of the Midwest and Southwest

Northern Goshawk
(NOR-thrn GAAS-haawk)

Northern goshawks are fierce hunters, using their flying ability and strong talons to take down prey. Goshawks are mostly gray, with a finely barred gray pattern on their bellies, and white eyebrows and gray caps on their heads. Falconers, people who train birds to hunt small animals such as rabbits, squirrels, or waterfowl have worked with goshawks for more than 2,000 years.

COLOR: Dark gray above, pale gray underneath
HEAD: Large; short, curved beak
SHAPE: Large size
RANGE: Across the United States

Peregrine Falcon
(PEH-ruh-gruhn FAL-kn)

Peregrine falcons are long-distance migrators. They hunt birds by swooping down onto them in midair. Peregrines were once nearly extinct, but are now making a recovery. From a distance, they appear mostly black and white. Up close, they are muscular-looking, with a yellow eye ring and short, thick, curved bill.

COLOR: Dark gray above, white and dark streaks underneath

HEAD: Flat; thick, yellow-and-gray curved bill; yellow eye ring

SHAPE: Medium to large size

RANGE: Across the United States

Prairie Falcon
(PREH-ree FAL-kn)

Prairie falcons are raptors that prefer wide-open spaces where they can search for small animals for food. They are sandy brown or gray with long, pointed wings; long tails; and white lines over their eyes. In some states, falconers are allowed to capture these birds as babies to train them—sometimes to hunt, but more often to ward off nuisance birds from property, acting like a flying scarecrow.

COLOR: Sandy brown to gray above; white line over eyes

HEAD: Large

SHAPE: Large size

RANGE: Great Plains and western United States

Sharp-Shinned Hawk
(SHAARP shind HAAWK)

The sharp-shinned hawk is the smallest hawk on the continent. They are identified by their distinct blue-gray color above and rust-ish bars across a white chest. They can also be noted by their long tails and short, rounded wings. Sharp-shinned hawks use their talons to pierce and hold onto prey.

COLOR: Blue to gray above; rust-ish bars across white chest

HEAD: Small; short, curved, yellow bill

SHAPE: Small hawk but medium-size bird

RANGE: Across the United States

Spotted Owl
(SPAA-tuhd owl)

The northern spotted owl lives in the Pacific Northwest. These birds are brown overall but have white spots on the head, back, and chest. They have an X pattern between their eyes. If spotted owls catch more than they can eat, they'll cache, or store, the food in a cool location for later.

COLOR: Brown overall, with white spots on back, head, and chest

HEAD: Large, round

SHAPE: Medium to large size

RANGE: Old-growth rain forests of the Pacific Northwest

American Avocet
(uh-MEH-rih-ken AA-vuh-set)

American avocets are graceful birds. They use their long legs to wade in water while swishing their long, thin, upturned bill back and forth and side to side in the water, searching for aquatic food—invertebrates (animals without backbones) such as worms or snails—to eat. Avocets have distinct black and white stripes and either gray- or rusty-colored heads. American avocets just one day old can walk, swim, and even dive.

COLOR: White below, black and white stripes above
HEAD: Gray- or rust-colored
SHAPE: Medium size
RANGE: Western parts of United States and Florida

American Oystercatcher
(uh-MEH-rih-ken OY-str-keh-chr)

American oystercatchers are shorebirds known for their red-yellow eyes and distinct red-orange bill. Oystercatchers are brown on top and white underneath. They eat only shellfish, so they typically stay near the ocean. Oystercatchers pry open shellfish by finding a mussel with its shell slightly open, then jabbing their bill into the crack to eat the shellfish. Or they will hammer the shell onto a rock to break it open.

COLOR: Brown on top; white underneath
HEAD: Black; red-yellow eyes
SHAPE: Medium size
RANGE: Atlantic coast and Gulf of Mexico

American Woodcock
(uh-MEH-rih-ken WUHD-kaak)

American woodcocks are unusually shaped shorebirds. Woodcocks are plump, with a short neck and legs, and a long bill they use to probe into the ground for food. They are a mixture of brown, black, and gray colors, making them hard to spot. A woodcock has eyes near the back of its skull.

COLOR: Mottled or mixed brown, black, and gray

HEAD: Large; short neck; long, straight bill

SHAPE: Medium size; plump and round

RANGE: Eastern half of the United States

Black-Necked Stilt
(BLAK nekt STILT)

Black-necked stilts live in wetlands. They are named "stilts" because of their long, stilt-like, rosy-pink legs. Stilts also have a long, thin, black bill. Their feathers are white on the bottom and black on top. Stilts have the longest leg-to-body-size proportion of any bird except flamingoes.

COLOR: White on the bottom and black on top; pink legs

HEAD: Round with a long, sharp bill

SHAPE: Medium size

RANGE: Western United States and the Southeast

California Gull
(ka-luh-FORN-yuh GUHL)

Despite the name, California gulls can be found throughout the western United States. They have a soft, white head, neck, and underside. Their long wings are gray with some black. California gulls are recognized for feasting on a plague of katydids and saving crops in Utah in 1848.

COLOR: White body with gray wings; black at back of wings

HEAD: Round; dark eyes

SHAPE: Medium size

RANGE: Western United States

Herring Gull
(HEH-ruhng GUHL)

Herring gulls are North America's most-observed gull. Herring gulls have a white head, neck, and belly with gray wings. They have some black at their wingtips. Herring gulls look strong, or barrel-chested. They have the ability to filter and drink sea or salt water.

COLOR: White head, neck, and belly; gray wings

HEAD: Round with yellow eyes; large bill

SHAPE: Large size

RANGE: Across the United States

Plover
(PLOH-vr)

Plovers are shorebirds that breed in the Arctic and migrate to the United States. They are found in mudflats and prairies, as well as along shorelines and beaches. Plovers have distinctly long legs and sharp bills. Adults leave the Arctic early in summer. Juveniles leave later, in summer or early fall.

COLOR: Male: distinct white crown down the neck with overall coloring of spotted gold, white, and black above and dark to black underneath; female: lighter brown overall and with brown and white cheeks

HEAD: Round; sharp bill

SHAPE: Medium size

RANGE: Mostly Central United States with rare sightings across the country

Spotted Sandpiper
(SPAA-tuhd SAND-pie-pr)

Spotted sandpipers are seen near freshwater, along the coast, and even in mountains up to 14,000 feet high! They often walk while crouched and are known to bob up and down. Spotted sandpiper females may mate with several males. It's the males who stay back and **incubate** the eggs, keeping them warm to hatch.

COLOR: Brown on top, white with dark patches underneath

HEAD: Long, sharp bill

SHAPE: Medium size

RANGE: Across North America

Willet
(WIH-lit)

Willets are large shorebirds known for their long legs; long, thick, straight bills; and mottled colors. They also have black and white stripes along each wing that are seen when flying. Willets pretend to be injured with a broken wing to lure predators away from their nests.

COLOR: Mottled brown and gray; white stripes on wings
HEAD: Round
SHAPE: Medium to large size
RANGE: Across the United States, except the East Coast and Pacific Northwest

Wilson's Phalarope
(WIL-sns FA-lr-owp)

Wilson's phalaropes are migrating shorebirds. They are gray overall with a cinnamon or rust color on their necks. They have long legs and a long, thin bill that help them wade through mudflats searching for food. Thousands of phalaropes put on a show in late summer, spinning around and stirring up the water so they can get nutrients to feed on.

COLOR: Grayish overall with rust color on neck
HEAD: Long, thin, straight bill
SHAPE: Medium size
RANGE: Western two-thirds of the United States and Great Lakes area

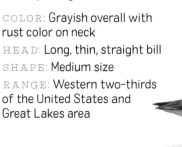

American Bittern

(uh-MEH-rih-ken BIH-turn)

American bitterns live near freshwater marshes. In winter, they may migrate to coastal waters that don't freeze. Bitterns are mostly brown and streaky-colored, which helps them blend in with reeds and bushes to avoid detection by predators. They are also known for their clacking, booming, and gulping sounds.

COLOR: Brown and streaky

HEAD: Long and thin; bill longer than head

SHAPE: Medium size

RANGE: Wetlands in most of the United States

American White Ibis

(uh-MEH-rih-ken WHY-t AI-buhs)

American white ibises live in wetlands in the Southeast. They are white with long red legs and a downward-sloping red bill. They have a small amount of red skin near their eyes. Baby ibises are born with straight bills, and at around 14 days old, the bill starts to curve.

COLOR: White bodies with black wing tips; red legs; red bill

HEAD: Red patch around eyes

SHAPE: Large size; football-shaped body

RANGE: Parts of the south-eastern United States, including all of Florida

American White Pelican
(uh-MEH-rih-ken WHY-t PEH-luh-kn)

American white pelicans are seen around lakes and wetlands. They are one of the largest birds in North America, with a wing span of 8 to 10 feet! American white pelicans have white bodies and white-and-black wings. Their large, yellow bills help them scoop up fish.

COLOR: All white, except black on parts of the wings

HEAD: Yellow bill that is much larger than the head

SHAPE: Very large size

RANGE: West of the Great Lakes and parts of the Southeast

Anhinga
(aan-HING-guh)

The anhinga is a large waterbird. Males are almost all black, with silvery streaks on their wings and back. Females are pale at the head, back, and breast, but have a dark belly. Anhingas are nicknamed "snake birds" because they swim through water, sometimes with only their snakelike necks showing.

COLOR: Male: mostly black with silver streaks; female: pale

HEAD: Long, thin; daggerlike, long bill

SHAPE: Large size

RANGE: Wetland areas of the southeastern United States

Common Loon
(KAA-muhn loon)

Common loons are found all over the United States. They are medium-size waterbirds that live in wetland areas. Loons have a black-and-white-striped collar and a black-and-white checkerboard shape on their back. Common loons need to run up to 30 yards across water before taking off.

COLOR: Black-and-white collar and back

HEAD: Powerful, pronounced bill; red eyes

SHAPE: Long body, curved neck

RANGE: Across the United States

Great Egret
(grayt EE-gruht)

Great Egrets are migrating birds that can be seen in most areas of the United States. They have long legs built for wading and a long, sharp bill made for stabbing fish while hunting. The great egret is the symbol of the National Audubon Society, an environmental organization.

COLOR: Almost all white with a yellow-gold bill

HEAD: Long, thin, flat

SHAPE: Large size; S-curved neck

RANGE: Wetlands in most of the United States in late summer or fall

Green-Backed Heron
(GREEN bakt HEH-ruhn)

The green-backed heron is a uniquely shaped waterbird. It is often seen standing, hunched over, on its long legs. Green-backed herons may appear dark from a distance but have a chestnut-colored chest and neck. Green-backed herons will drop bread or an insect onto the water to lure up fish.

COLOR: Green back and crown; chestnut neck and breast

HEAD: Flat; long, daggerlike bill

SHAPE: Medium size

RANGE: Wetlands across the United States

Pied-Billed Grebe
(PYE-d bild GREEB)

Pied-billed grebes are waterbirds known for their ultra-thick bills. They are chunky-shaped and have no tail. Breeding pied-billed grebes have a black stripe on their bills. Nonbreeding ones have a brown neck. *Grebe*, in Latin, means "feet at buttocks," which is where their feet are.

COLOR: Mostly brown; crown and throat areas turn black in summer

HEAD: Black; thick bill

SHAPE: Medium size

RANGE: Across the United States

Sandhill Crane
(SAND-hil KRAYN)

Sandhill cranes are large, elegant waterbirds that can be seen in wetlands and fields. Sandhill cranes have long legs, a long neck, and wide wings. They are gray to white overall, but their legs are black. Sandhill cranes gather together and fly in groups of hundreds—or even thousands.

COLOR: Gray overall; red skin on face

HEAD: Small; long, straight bill

SHAPE: Very large size; long legs, long neck

RANGE: Most of North America

American Widgeon
(uh-MEH-rih-ken WIH-jn)

American widgeons are dazzling ducks. Males have a green stripe behind their eyes and white caps on their heads. Females are brown overall with some gray. Widgeons typically have their heads tucked down, looking as if they have no neck. Females make small depressions in the ground in which to nest.

COLOR: Male: brownish with green patch behind eye; female: mottled brown

HEAD: Round; white bill and white cap on head

SHAPE: Medium to large size

RANGE: Across the United States

Bufflehead Duck
(BUH-fuhl-hed DUHK)

Buffleheads are migrating ducks. They are small for a duck, but with a large, bulbous-shaped head and a short bill. Unlike most ducks, Buffleheads stay with the same mate for several years. They build their nests in holes dug by northern flickers and pileated woodpeckers.

COLOR: Male: dark black, white belly, white patch on head with glossy green-and-purple patch; female: brown with white patch on cheeks

HEAD: Large

SHAPE: Medium size

RANGE: Coastal United States in winter; inland and Canada in summer

Canvasback Duck
(KAN-vuhs-bak DUHK)

Canvasbacks are striking ducks that can be found across the United States. Canvasback ducks hold their heads high in the water. Males have a chestnut-colored head with a black chest, white body, and black rear. Females are pale brown and gray. Females sometimes lay their eggs in other canvasbacks' nests in hopes that the other bird will take responsibility to incubate them.

COLOR: Male: black, white, and chestnut; female: brown and gray

HEAD: Sloping forehead; thick neck; long bill

SHAPE: Large size

RANGE: Lakes and ponds all over the United States

Common Gallinule
(KAA-muhn GAL-luh-nool)

Gallinules are known for the bright red covering over their forehead and bill. They also have long yellow legs, a thin neck, and thin bill. Gallinules are charcoal gray with white on their outer tails and sides. The gallinule's long toes help it walk on mud or even on water plants.

COLOR: Charcoal body; bright red shield on forehead

HEAD: Small; thin neck

SHAPE: Medium size

RANGE: Eastern half of the United States, the Southwest, and California

Common Goldeneye
(KAA-muhn GOHLD-uhn-eye)

Common goldeneyes are ducks seen across the United States. They have white patches on their wings and distinct golden eyes. Males have an iridescent green head with a distinct round white spot behind the bill. They nest in trees and abandoned buildings anywhere from 5 to 60 feet off the ground. The chicks leave their nest at one day old, dropping from the nest when Mom calls from below.

COLOR: Black and white, with yellow or golden eyes; female: brown head

HEAD: Triangular shape

SHAPE: Medium to large size

RANGE: Across the United States, except extreme south

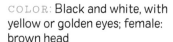

Common Merganser
(KAA-muhn mr-GAN-sr)

Common mergansers are large ducks found in forested areas with lakes and rivers. Males have white bodies, green heads, and a red bill. Females have a gray body and cinnamon-brown head. Merganser chicks leave their nests at around one day old and start foraging for insects on their own.

COLOR: Male: white head, green body; female: gray body, cinnamon-brown head

HEAD: Large, long, flat; long bill

SHAPE: Large size

RANGE: Most of the United States

Gadwall
(GAD-waal)

Gadwalls are elegant ducks that can be identified by their large, square-shaped heads. Male gadwalls are gray to brown with a patch of black at their rump. Females have an orange edge to their dark bill. Gadwalls sometimes steal from a diving duck as it surfaces with food.

COLOR: Male: gray to brown with black patch at the back; female: brown overall with orange on the bill

HEAD: Large; steep forehead; thin bill

SHAPE: Large size

RANGE: Across the United States

Northern Pintail
(NOR-thrn PIN-tayl)

Northern pintails are named for their long, pin-like tail that sticks up out of the water as the duck submerges its head while feeding. Males have a long neck, white breast, and a white neck stripe. Females are spotted brown overall. Northern pintails can fly a distance of up to 1,800 miles—nonstop!

COLOR: Male: brown head, white-gray-and-black body; female: mostly brown

HEAD: Round

SHAPE: Large size

RANGE: Wetlands across the United States

Northern Shoveler
(NOR-thrn SHUH-vuh-lr)

Northern shovelers are named for their spoon, or shovel-shaped, bill. The bill also has tiny projections on it to help separate the food from the water. Males grab attention due to their green neck and head and very long black bill. Females are mostly brown.

COLOR: Male: green head and neck; female: mostly brown, with blue shoulder patch

HEAD: Long, shovel-shaped bill

SHAPE: Large size

RANGE: Across the United States

Ruddy Duck
(RUH-dee DUHK)

Ruddy ducks are compact-size ducks. Breeding males have a distinct wide-shaped blue bill and chestnut-colored body. Females are mostly brownish overall. Ruddy ducks often have their tails sticking up. Their eggs are larger than any other duck's eggs compared to their body size. Their call is also distinct: a long, loud rhythmic series of sounds defined as whoops, coos, gulps, and chuckling chatter.

COLOR: Breeding male: chestnut body; nonbreeding male: ruddy color and without the blue bill; female: tan-brown

HEAD: Large; large, flat bill

SHAPE: Medium size; tail sticks up

RANGE: Across the United States

Snow Goose
(snoh goos)

Snow geese are migrating birds that spend their winters in North America. They live in or near wetlands and fields. Their distinct white bodies and loud calls makes them easy to identify. Snow geese fly great distances, but they can also walk a long way, up to 50 miles per day.

COLOR: Almost all white with some black outside feathers

HEAD: Large head and bill; long neck

SHAPE: Large size

RANGE: Winters in North America

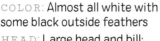

Trumpeter Swan
(TRUHM-puh-tr swaan)

Trumpeter swans are North America's largest waterfowl. They are almost all white. Trumpeter swans can grow to 6 feet long and weigh up to 25 pounds. It takes about 100 yards of open water for the swans to build up enough running speed that they can fly.

COLOR: Almost all white

HEAD: Large; black bill

SHAPE: Very large size; long neck

RANGE: Northern parts of the United States

Wood Duck
(wuhd duhk)

Wood ducks are simply gorgeous. Males have a green-crested head and a chestnut breast, along with splashes of white, black, and brown. Females are a warm brown with patches of blue and white. Females sometimes lay eggs in other ducks' nests, leaving the chicks to be raised by another duck.

COLOR: Male: glossy-green head, white stripes, chestnut, and brown; female: gray and brown with whitish, spotted breast

HEAD: Box shaped, with crest

SHAPE: Medium to large size

RANGE: Across the United States

My Field Notebook

How to Use This Notebook

This field notebook gives you a place to take notes on your expeditions so you can create a record of all the birds you've seen, when you saw them, and where you were. Afterward, you can compare and contrast as you keep your running list.

The name of the bird, date, and location spotted is important to record. So is the weather that day and whether it could have affected the bird. There is also a line to describe the bird.

There are also check boxes for pictures and sketches. Did you take any or make any? That information could be noted.

The log entries include four lines for any special notes. These could include a full description of the location—such as a preserve, refuge, or national park. Were you with a group that day? Who was the leader of your group? Those are just a few ideas to get you started.

Lifers are birds you are seeing for the very first time that day. This is an exciting moment! Many birders like to note what bird it was and where they saw it. You may also want to add into your journal whether that bird is native or unique to that habitat. Lifers are a big deal among birders.

LOG NUMBER: .... DATE: ....

SPECIES NAME: ....

LOCATION: ....

WEATHER: ....

DESCRIPTION: ....

OBSERVATIONS: ....

PICTURE TAKEN ☐   WAS IT A LIFER? ☐

NOTES: ....

....

....

....

SKETCH

LOG NUMBER: .... DATE: ....

SPECIES NAME: ....

LOCATION: ....

WEATHER: ....

DESCRIPTION: ....

OBSERVATIONS: ....

PICTURE TAKEN ☐   WAS IT A LIFER? ☐

NOTES: ....

....

....

....

SKETCH

LOG NUMBER: .... DATE: ....

SPECIES NAME: ....

LOCATION: ....

WEATHER: ....

DESCRIPTION: ....

OBSERVATIONS: ....

PICTURE TAKEN ☐   WAS IT A LIFER? ☐

NOTES: ....

....

....

....

| SKETCH |
| |
| |

LOG NUMBER: .... DATE: ....

SPECIES NAME: ....

LOCATION: ....

WEATHER: ....

DESCRIPTION: ....

OBSERVATIONS: ....

PICTURE TAKEN ☐   WAS IT A LIFER? ☐

NOTES: ....

....

....

....

| SKETCH |
| |
| |

LOG NUMBER: .... DATE: ....

SPECIES NAME: ....

LOCATION: ....

WEATHER: ....

DESCRIPTION: ....

OBSERVATIONS: ....

PICTURE TAKEN ☐   WAS IT A LIFER? ☐

NOTES: ....

....

....

....

SKETCH

LOG NUMBER: .... DATE: ....

SPECIES NAME: ....

LOCATION: ....

WEATHER: ....

DESCRIPTION: ....

OBSERVATIONS: ....

PICTURE TAKEN ☐   WAS IT A LIFER? ☐

NOTES: ....

....

....

....

SKETCH

LOG NUMBER: .... DATE: ....

SPECIES NAME: ....

LOCATION: ....

WEATHER: ....

DESCRIPTION: ....

OBSERVATIONS: ....

PICTURE TAKEN ☐   WAS IT A LIFER? ☐

NOTES: ....

....

....

....

SKETCH

LOG NUMBER: .... DATE: ....

SPECIES NAME: ....

LOCATION: ....

WEATHER: ....

DESCRIPTION: ....

OBSERVATIONS: ....

PICTURE TAKEN ☐   WAS IT A LIFER? ☐

NOTES: ....

....

....

....

SKETCH

LOG NUMBER: .... DATE: ....

SPECIES NAME: ....

LOCATION: ....

WEATHER: ....

DESCRIPTION: ....

OBSERVATIONS: ....

PICTURE TAKEN ☐   WAS IT A LIFER? ☐

NOTES: ....

....

....

....

SKETCH

LOG NUMBER: .... DATE: ....

SPECIES NAME: ....

LOCATION: ....

WEATHER: ....

DESCRIPTION: ....

OBSERVATIONS: ....

PICTURE TAKEN ☐   WAS IT A LIFER? ☐

NOTES: ....

....

....

....

SKETCH

LOG NUMBER: .... DATE: ....

SPECIES NAME: ....

LOCATION: ....

WEATHER: ....

DESCRIPTION: ....

OBSERVATIONS: ....

PICTURE TAKEN ☐   WAS IT A LIFER? ☐

NOTES: ....

....

....

....

SKETCH

LOG NUMBER: .... DATE: ....

SPECIES NAME: ....

LOCATION: ....

WEATHER: ....

DESCRIPTION: ....

OBSERVATIONS: ....

PICTURE TAKEN ☐   WAS IT A LIFER? ☐

NOTES: ....

....

....

....

SKETCH

LOG NUMBER: .... DATE: ....

SPECIES NAME: ....

LOCATION: ....

WEATHER: ....

DESCRIPTION: ....

OBSERVATIONS: ....

PICTURE TAKEN ☐   WAS IT A LIFER? ☐

NOTES: ....

....

....

....

SKETCH

LOG NUMBER: .... DATE: ....

SPECIES NAME: ....

LOCATION: ....

WEATHER: ....

DESCRIPTION: ....

OBSERVATIONS: ....

PICTURE TAKEN ☐   WAS IT A LIFER? ☐

NOTES: ....

....

....

....

SKETCH

LOG NUMBER: .... DATE: ....

SPECIES NAME: ....

LOCATION: ....

WEATHER: ....

DESCRIPTION: ....

OBSERVATIONS: ....

PICTURE TAKEN ☐   WAS IT A LIFER? ☐

NOTES: ....

....

....

....

SKETCH

LOG NUMBER: .... DATE: ....

SPECIES NAME: ....

LOCATION: ....

WEATHER: ....

DESCRIPTION: ....

OBSERVATIONS: ....

PICTURE TAKEN ☐   WAS IT A LIFER? ☐

NOTES: ....

....

....

....

SKETCH

LOG NUMBER: .... DATE: ....

SPECIES NAME: ....

LOCATION: ....

WEATHER: ....

DESCRIPTION: ....

OBSERVATIONS: ....

PICTURE TAKEN ☐   WAS IT A LIFER? ☐

NOTES: ....

....

....

....

SKETCH

LOG NUMBER: .... DATE: ....

SPECIES NAME: ....

LOCATION: ....

WEATHER: ....

DESCRIPTION: ....

OBSERVATIONS: ....

PICTURE TAKEN ☐   WAS IT A LIFER? ☐

NOTES: ....

....

....

....

SKETCH

LOG NUMBER: .... DATE: ....

SPECIES NAME: ....

LOCATION: ....

WEATHER: ....

DESCRIPTION: ....

OBSERVATIONS: ....

PICTURE TAKEN ☐   WAS IT A LIFER? ☐

NOTES: ....

....

....

....

SKETCH

LOG NUMBER: .... DATE: ....

SPECIES NAME: ....

LOCATION: ....

WEATHER: ....

DESCRIPTION: ....

OBSERVATIONS: ....

PICTURE TAKEN ☐   WAS IT A LIFER? ☐

NOTES: ....

....

....

....

SKETCH

LOG NUMBER: .... DATE: ....

SPECIES NAME: ....

LOCATION: ....

WEATHER: ....

DESCRIPTION: ....

OBSERVATIONS: ....

PICTURE TAKEN ☐   WAS IT A LIFER? ☐

NOTES: ....

....

....

....

SKETCH

LOG NUMBER: .... DATE: ....

SPECIES NAME: ....

LOCATION: ....

WEATHER: ....

DESCRIPTION: ....

OBSERVATIONS: ....

PICTURE TAKEN ☐   WAS IT A LIFER? ☐

NOTES: ....

....

....

....

SKETCH

LOG NUMBER: .... DATE: ....

SPECIES NAME: ....

LOCATION: ....

WEATHER: ....

DESCRIPTION: ....

OBSERVATIONS: ....

PICTURE TAKEN ☐   WAS IT A LIFER? ☐

NOTES: ....

....

....

....

SKETCH

LOG NUMBER: .... DATE: ....

SPECIES NAME: ....

LOCATION: ....

WEATHER: ....

DESCRIPTION: ....

OBSERVATIONS: ....

PICTURE TAKEN ☐   WAS IT A LIFER? ☐

NOTES: ....

....

....

....

SKETCH

LOG NUMBER: _____ DATE: _____

SPECIES NAME: _____

LOCATION: _____

WEATHER: _____

DESCRIPTION: _____

OBSERVATIONS: _____

PICTURE TAKEN ☐   WAS IT A LIFER? ☐

NOTES: _____

_____

_____

_____

SKETCH

LOG NUMBER: .... DATE: ....

SPECIES NAME: ....

LOCATION: ....

WEATHER: ....

DESCRIPTION: ....

OBSERVATIONS: ....

PICTURE TAKEN ☐   WAS IT A LIFER? ☐

NOTES: ....

....

....

....

SKETCH

LOG NUMBER: .... DATE: ....

SPECIES NAME: ....

LOCATION: ....

WEATHER: ....

DESCRIPTION: ....

OBSERVATIONS: ....

PICTURE TAKEN ☐   WAS IT A LIFER? ☐

NOTES: ....

....

....

....

SKETCH

LOG NUMBER: .... DATE: ....

SPECIES NAME: ....

LOCATION: ....

WEATHER: ....

DESCRIPTION: ....

OBSERVATIONS: ....

PICTURE TAKEN ☐   WAS IT A LIFER? ☐

NOTES: ....

....

....

....

SKETCH

LOG NUMBER: .... DATE: ....

SPECIES NAME: ....

LOCATION: ....

WEATHER: ....

DESCRIPTION: ....

OBSERVATIONS: ....

PICTURE TAKEN ☐   WAS IT A LIFER? ☐

NOTES: ....

....

....

....

SKETCH

LOG NUMBER: .... DATE: ....

SPECIES NAME: ....

LOCATION: ....

WEATHER: ....

DESCRIPTION: ....

OBSERVATIONS: ....

PICTURE TAKEN ☐   WAS IT A LIFER? ☐

NOTES: ....

....

....

....

SKETCH

LOG NUMBER: .... DATE: ....

SPECIES NAME: ....

LOCATION: ....

WEATHER: ....

DESCRIPTION: ....

OBSERVATIONS: ....

PICTURE TAKEN ☐   WAS IT A LIFER? ☐

NOTES: ....

....

....

....

SKETCH

LOG NUMBER: .... DATE: ....

SPECIES NAME: ....

LOCATION: ....

WEATHER: ....

DESCRIPTION: ....

OBSERVATIONS: ....

PICTURE TAKEN ☐   WAS IT A LIFER? ☐

NOTES: ....

....

....

....

SKETCH

LOG NUMBER: .... DATE: ....

SPECIES NAME: ....

LOCATION: ....

WEATHER: ....

DESCRIPTION: ....

OBSERVATIONS: ....

PICTURE TAKEN ☐   WAS IT A LIFER? ☐

NOTES: ....

....

....

....

SKETCH

LOG NUMBER: _____ DATE: _____

SPECIES NAME: _____

LOCATION: _____

WEATHER: _____

DESCRIPTION: _____

OBSERVATIONS: _____

PICTURE TAKEN ☐   WAS IT A LIFER? ☐

NOTES: _____

....

....

....

SKETCH

LOG NUMBER: .... DATE: ....

SPECIES NAME: ....

LOCATION: ....

WEATHER: ....

DESCRIPTION: ....

OBSERVATIONS: ....

PICTURE TAKEN ☐   WAS IT A LIFER? ☐

NOTES: ....

....

....

....

SKETCH

LOG NUMBER: .... DATE: ....

SPECIES NAME: ....

LOCATION: ....

WEATHER: ....

DESCRIPTION: ....

OBSERVATIONS: ....

PICTURE TAKEN ☐   WAS IT A LIFER? ☐

NOTES: ....

....

....

....

SKETCH

LOG NUMBER: .... DATE: ....

SPECIES NAME: ....

LOCATION: ....

WEATHER: ....

DESCRIPTION: ....

OBSERVATIONS: ....

PICTURE TAKEN ☐   WAS IT A LIFER? ☐

NOTES: ....

....

....

....

SKETCH

LOG NUMBER: .... DATE: ....

SPECIES NAME: ....

LOCATION: ....

WEATHER: ....

DESCRIPTION: ....

OBSERVATIONS: ....

PICTURE TAKEN ☐   WAS IT A LIFER? ☐

NOTES: ....

....

....

....

| SKETCH |
| |
| |

LOG NUMBER: .... DATE: ....

SPECIES NAME: ....

LOCATION: ....

WEATHER: ....

DESCRIPTION: ....

OBSERVATIONS: ....

PICTURE TAKEN ☐   WAS IT A LIFER? ☐

NOTES: ....

....

....

....

SKETCH

LOG NUMBER: .... DATE: ....

SPECIES NAME: ....

LOCATION: ....

WEATHER: ....

DESCRIPTION: ....

OBSERVATIONS: ....

PICTURE TAKEN ☐   WAS IT A LIFER? ☐

NOTES: ....

....

....

....

SKETCH

LOG NUMBER: .... DATE: ....

SPECIES NAME: ....

LOCATION: ....

WEATHER: ....

DESCRIPTION: ....

OBSERVATIONS: ....

PICTURE TAKEN ☐   WAS IT A LIFER? ☐

NOTES: ....

....

....

....

SKETCH

LOG NUMBER: .... DATE: ....

SPECIES NAME: ....

LOCATION: ....

WEATHER: ....

DESCRIPTION: ....

OBSERVATIONS: ....

PICTURE TAKEN ☐   WAS IT A LIFER? ☐

NOTES: ....

....

....

....

SKETCH

LOG NUMBER: .... DATE: ....

SPECIES NAME: ....

LOCATION: ....

WEATHER: ....

DESCRIPTION: ....

OBSERVATIONS: ....

PICTURE TAKEN ☐   WAS IT A LIFER? ☐

NOTES: ....

....

....

....

SKETCH

LOG NUMBER: .... DATE: ....

SPECIES NAME: ....

LOCATION: ....

WEATHER: ....

DESCRIPTION: ....

OBSERVATIONS: ....

PICTURE TAKEN ☐   WAS IT A LIFER? ☐

NOTES: ....

....

....

....

SKETCH

LOG NUMBER: .... DATE: ....

SPECIES NAME: ....

LOCATION: ....

WEATHER: ....

DESCRIPTION: ....

OBSERVATIONS: ....

PICTURE TAKEN ☐   WAS IT A LIFER? ☐

NOTES: ....

....

....

....

SKETCH

LOG NUMBER: _____ DATE: _____

SPECIES NAME: _____

LOCATION: _____

WEATHER: _____

DESCRIPTION: _____

OBSERVATIONS: _____

PICTURE TAKEN ☐   WAS IT A LIFER? ☐

NOTES: _____

_____

_____

_____

SKETCH

LOG NUMBER: .... DATE: ....

SPECIES NAME: ....

LOCATION: ....

WEATHER: ....

DESCRIPTION: ....

OBSERVATIONS: ....

PICTURE TAKEN ☐   WAS IT A LIFER? ☐

NOTES: ....

....

....

....

SKETCH

LOG NUMBER: .... DATE: ....

SPECIES NAME: ....

LOCATION: ....

WEATHER: ....

DESCRIPTION: ....

OBSERVATIONS: ....

PICTURE TAKEN ☐   WAS IT A LIFER? ☐

NOTES: ....

....

....

....

SKETCH

LOG NUMBER: .... DATE: ....

SPECIES NAME: ....

LOCATION: ....

WEATHER: ....

DESCRIPTION: ....

OBSERVATIONS: ....

PICTURE TAKEN ☐   WAS IT A LIFER? ☐

NOTES: ....

....

....

....

SKETCH

LOG NUMBER: .... DATE: ....

SPECIES NAME: ....

LOCATION: ....

WEATHER: ....

DESCRIPTION: ....

OBSERVATIONS: ....

PICTURE TAKEN ☐   WAS IT A LIFER? ☐

NOTES: ....

....

....

....

SKETCH

LOG NUMBER: .... DATE: ....

SPECIES NAME: ....

LOCATION: ....

WEATHER: ....

DESCRIPTION: ....

OBSERVATIONS: ....

PICTURE TAKEN ☐   WAS IT A LIFER? ☐

NOTES: ....

....

....

....

SKETCH

LOG NUMBER: .... DATE: ....

SPECIES NAME: ....

LOCATION: ....

WEATHER: ....

DESCRIPTION: ....

OBSERVATIONS: ....

PICTURE TAKEN ☐   WAS IT A LIFER? ☐

NOTES: ....

....

....

....

SKETCH

LOG NUMBER: .... DATE: ....

SPECIES NAME: ....

LOCATION: ....

WEATHER: ....

DESCRIPTION: ....

OBSERVATIONS: ....

PICTURE TAKEN ☐   WAS IT A LIFER? ☐

NOTES: ....

....

....

....

SKETCH

LOG NUMBER: .... DATE: ....

SPECIES NAME: ....

LOCATION: ....

WEATHER: ....

DESCRIPTION: ....

OBSERVATIONS: ....

PICTURE TAKEN ☐   WAS IT A LIFER? ☐

NOTES: ....

....

....

....

SKETCH

LOG NUMBER: .... DATE: ....

SPECIES NAME: ....

LOCATION: ....

WEATHER: ....

DESCRIPTION: ....

OBSERVATIONS: ....

PICTURE TAKEN ☐   WAS IT A LIFER? ☐

NOTES: ....

....

....

....

SKETCH

LOG NUMBER: .... DATE: ....

SPECIES NAME: ....

LOCATION: ....

WEATHER: ....

DESCRIPTION: ....

OBSERVATIONS: ....

PICTURE TAKEN ☐   WAS IT A LIFER? ☐

NOTES: ....

....

....

....

SKETCH

Good Luck, Birders!

Congratulations! You are well on your way to becoming an official birder. There are so many places to go and so many birds to see. North America is a great place to start. But the birds of Asia, Australia, and Africa, among other locations, are amazing, too! I truly hope you enjoy every minute of your newfound hobby. Pass the knowledge and enthusiasm along. Take others with you and learn together to appreciate all you can about our planet's wonderful birds. Bring this book with you when you go, have the best of times, and good luck!

Glossary

adaptation: When an animal modifies or changes over time to fit and survive in its environment

adult: A fully grown person or animal

altitude: The height or elevation of an object relative to sea level

anatomy: The bodily structure or inner workings of a person or animal

anting: When birds actively rub ants onto their feathers and skin or let ants crawl on them

aquatic: Related to water

avian: Related to birds

behavior: The way an animal reacts in response to its environment

breast: An animal's chest

cache: To store away or hide something, such as food, for future use

carnivore: A person or animal that eats meat

carrion: Flesh or meat of dead animals

cartilage: Tough, semitransparent connective tissue

crest: A tuft of feathers on a bird's head

diopter: The power of a lens or curved mirror in a pair of binoculars

elongated: Long or stretched out, in association with the object's width

endothermic: An animal able to generate its own body heat

estuaries: The mouths of large rivers, where the ocean's salt water meets the river's freshwater

evolved: To change slowly over time, often into a better adapted or more complex state

extinct: An animal no longer in existence, or in existence in that area

flank: The side of an animal's body

flyways: Migration routes birds fly between nesting and wintering areas

gaping: Opening a hole

habitat: The natural home of a plant or animal

hawking: A way birds catch flying insects with their bills

hover: Staying in one place while flying, often associated with hummingbirds

incubate: When a bird sits on eggs to keep them warm

juvenile: A not-fully-developed, or younger, animal or person

kiting: Birder term for a form of hovering in one place and using the wind to stay aloft, usually associated with hunting for prey

migration: The seasonal movement of animals from one region to another

mottled: Spots or smears of color

nomadic: Moving or wandering from place to place

omnivore: A person or animal that feeds on plants and meat

range: The specific areas where an animal can live in their lifetime, mostly due to climate

raptor: A bird of prey, such as an eagle, hawk, or owl

residents: People or animals that live in a certain area

resources: Materials needed to survive in one area

rump: The lower back of a bird

sea stack: Pillar of rock detached from the shore by waves

species: A group of living organisms with similar characteristics and genes

spherical: Like a sphere, or round

theropods: Carnivorous, two-footed dinosaurs

tundras: Rolling, treeless plains typical of arctic and subarctic regions; can occur further south at high elevations

undulating: Smoothly and repeatedly rising and falling while flying

urban: Characteristic of a city or town

vertebrate: An animal with a backbone or spinal column

wattle: Flap of skin hanging under the chin of a wild turkey

Resources

There are many great places on the internet to learn more about birds. These sources will also help you identify birds based on field marks and songs. Here are some places to start.

Bird Watcher's Digest

BirdWatchersDigest.com

The online site of *Bird Watcher's Digest* and other magazines provides bird-watchers with the world's greatest bird magazine.

Chirp! Bird Songs & Calls USA

Apps.Apple.com/us/app/chirp-bird-songs-calls-usa /id364891918

This app has more than 300 bird songs for you to listen to!

National Audubon Society

Audubon.org

The National Audubon Society focuses solely on protecting birds and their habitats. You'll find bird identification, facts, and outings, too.

The Cornell Lab of Ornithology

Birds.Cornell.edu

Here you can find a ton of bird identifications and related information.

The Cornell Lab of Ornithology—eBird

eBird.org

This website allows you to find birds, share information, and track birds, including lifers and other unusual sightings.

The Cornell Lab of Ornithology—Merlin

Merlin.AllAboutBirds.org

This app "wizard" can instantly identify North American birds, and birds across the other continents as well!

References

BOOKS

Alderfer, Jonathan, and Noah Strycker. *National Geographic Backyard Guide to the Birds of North America*, 2nd ed. National Geographic: Washington, DC, 2019.

Kroodsma, Donald. *The Backyard Birdsong Guide (Eastern and Central North America)*. Princeton, NJ: Princeton University Press/The Cornell Lab Publishing Group, 2008.

_____. *The Backyard Birdsong Guide (Western North America)*. Princeton, NJ: Princeton Univeristy Press/ The Cornell Lab Publishing Group, 2008.

WEBSITES

Birds & Blooms. "Birding." Last modified 2021. birdsandblooms.com/birding.

Sibley, David Allen. "Sibley Guides." Last modified 2021. sibleyguides.com/bird-info.

The Spruce. "Wild Birds." Last modified 2021. thespruce.com/wild-birds-4127712.

Index

About the Author

Author MIKE GRAF has taught fourth and fifth grade for 10 years, as well as GATE education, in San Luis Obispo, California. He also taught education and child development classes at Chico State University in California. In addition, Mike has been a television weathercaster off and on for nearly 30 years.

Mike has written more than 95 books for children, families, and teachers. He enjoys writing about national parks, weather and storm chasing, dinosaur digs, animal encounters, ghost towns, geography, STEM fields, and more.

Visit Mike's website, MikeGrafAuthor.com, to see more of his work.

CPSIA information can be obtained
at www.ICGtesting.com
Printed in the USA
LVHW020743290522
720009LV00001B/1